Intercede For and With Your Family

Intercede For and With Your Family

By
Archie Parrish

SERVE INTERNATIONAL • ATLANTA, GEORGIA

Dedication

"For these children we prayed, and the LORD has granted us our petition, which we asked of Him. Therefore, we also have lent them to the LORD; as long as they live they shall be lent to the LORD." (Parrish paraphrase of 1 Samuel 1:27-28).

Forty-six years ago, in response to prayer, God brought Jean and I together to start our family. As we prayed together God gave us John, then Anne and Jane. Over the years, we continued to pray, and God brought Fred to Anne, Phylis to John, and Bill to Jane. Then, to Fred and Anne, God gave Cyrus; to John and Phylis, God gave Jesse and Amanda; and to Bill and Jane, God gave Morgan Grace. To this day, every time Jean and I eat a meal, we pray for each of our children, their mates and our grandchildren. To these eleven people, who are proof that God answers prayer for and with your family, I dedicate this book.

Table of Contents

Acknowledgments

I am deeply grateful to Rev. Don Kistler, of Sola Dei Gloria Publications for his collection of Puritan writers in the *Godly Family, A series of essays on the duties of parents and children.* This was very helpful in the writing of this book. Also, I am grateful to Rev. L. R. Shelton, Jr., Pastor of Mt. Zion Bible Church, Pensacola, FL. His ministry as publisher of the *Free Grace Broadcaster* provides inexpensive, hard-to-find, biblically sound material that "humbles the pride of man, exalts the grace of God in salvation and promotes real holiness in heart and life." I have spent so much time in the materials provided by these two men that it is hard for me to tell where their thoughts stop and my thinking begins. Charles Colson's writings I always find stimulating. For writing ***Intercede For and With Your Family***, his book, *How Now Shall We Live?*, chapter 33, "God's Training Ground," was especially helpful.

Before You Begin

Intercede For and With Your Family is written to strengthen godly families in today's hostile culture. It is designed to be a training manual and, when properly used, it will help you achieve God's purpose for your family through kingdom-focused prayer. The material included here is to be used for stage II of the Kingdom Campaign,[1] a movement aimed at building a super-critical mass composed of 120 kingdom intercessors in 120 local churches in 120 metro areas in North America. The objective of the Kingdom Campaign is twofold: to equip believers to develop the daily discipline of kingdom-focused prayer, and to encourage them to multiply after their kind that is, to train others to do the same.

This book looks at God's design for families. The truth presented is essential for all people, regardless of their

---

[1] If you have not read the free sixteen-page booklet, *The Kingdom Campaign* (available from Serve International, 4646 N. Shallowford Rd., Suite 200, Atlanta, GA 30338), please do so now. It comes with *Improve Your Prayer Life* and describes the best process for learning the material in this book and implementing a supercritical mass of kingdom-focused prayer in your local church. It will explain the foundations upon which the Kingdom Campaign is built, and will also show the role of the other books in the Kingdom Campaign series: *Improve Your Prayer Life, Intercede For and With Your Family; Invigorate Your Church; Impact Your World;* and *Ignite Your Leadership* (Leader's Guide for the series).

present familial situation. Socially you may be in a traditional nuclear family, or you may be a single person who has never been married; you may be a divorced person living alone, or remarried with a blended family. You may have been widowed; you may never have had children, or your children may be adults with their own families. If you are trusting Christ, spiritually you are in the family of God and all other Christians are your brothers and sisters. Whether you are a man, woman, boy or girl, no matter what your situation, you can benefit from learning more about God's plan for you. As you read this book, pray for members of both your physical and your spiritual family.

This book looks at God's design for families. The truth presented is essential for all people, regardless of their present familial situation. If you are trusting Christ, spiritually you are in the family of God and all other Christians are your brothers and sisters. Whether you are a man, woman, boy or girl, no matter what your situation, you can benefit from learning more about God's plan for you. As you read this book, pray for members of both your physical and your spiritual family.

Intercede For and With Your Family seeks to build on the process that was begun in *Improve Your Prayer Life*. If you worked through that text first, you will already be praying daily with a kingdom focus for 15 minutes. In this book, you will be encouraged to add another 15 minutes to that time—for a total of 30 minutes daily. To do that, you will need to plan time to work through the material in this book as well as to plan time each day to pray. Be sure to read the introductory remarks of the *Discussion Guide* (pages 99 through 117) before you begin reading the text on page 15! You will find directions there for working through the text and for continuing to develop the daily discipline of kingdom-focused prayer.

Touched by an Angel

Suppose God sent you an angel today who tells you he was the angel who destroyed the firstborn sons in Egypt, sparing only the houses where he saw blood sprinkled on the doorpost. When you inquire as to his present mission, he informs you that God has sent him to answer Jeremiah's prayer, *"Pour out Your fury on the Gentiles, who do not know You, and on the families who do not call on Your name; for they have eaten up Jacob, devoured him and consumed him, and made his dwelling place desolate."*[2] The angel has come to earth this time to warn all professing Christian families that, in 90 days, God will pour out His fury on all who do not call upon the Lord in daily prayer. You have 90 days to put your house in order. What would you do?

God's will is that families pray together. Someone once said, "A family without prayer is like a house without a roof, open and exposed to all the storms of Heaven." The Apostle James tells us, *"Every good gift and every perfect gift is from above, and comes down from the Father of lights, with whom there is no variation or shadow of*

---

[2] Jeremiah 10:25

13

turning."[3] All our family comforts and temporal mercies come from the gracious hand of the Lord, and the best we can do in return is to gratefully acknowledge this fact, together as a family. Regular family worship teaches children, and reminds adults, about the habit of having a thankful heart before God.

Remember the Prayer Survey you took at the beginning of *Improve Your Prayer Life*? It pointed to a gap between what we believe, and what we do. In *Intercede For and With Your Family*, we are still trying to close that sanctification gap. Please take my challenge for the next ninety days—to prayerfully work through the material in this book as a member of a four-person fireteam. If you do, I know you will experience increased fruitfulness and joy!

God's will is that families pray together. Someone once said, "A family without prayer is like a house without a roof, open and exposed to all the storms of Heaven." All our family comforts and temporal mercies come from the gracious hand of the Lord, and the best we can do in return is to gratefully acknowledge this fact, together as a family.

•••••

---

[3] James 1:17

14

The Family's Present Plight

David Popenoe predicts, "If the family trends of recent decades are extended into the future, the result will be not only growing uncertainty within marriage, but the gradual elimination of marriage in favor of casual liaisons, oriented adult expressions, and self-fulfillment. The problem with this scenario is that children will be harmed, adults will probably be no happier, and the social order could collapse."[4]

Charles Colson in *How Now Shall We Live?* tells us, "This systematic deconstruction of the oldest, most basic social institution is a prime cause of the social chaos in America in recent decades."[5]   He continues, "Typically our efforts are reactive rather than proactive, largely because we have failed to confront the underlying worldview assumptions."[6] Then he marshals these facts:

Children in single-parent families are six times more likely to be poor, and half the single mothers in the United States live below the poverty line. Children of divorce suffer intense grief, which often lasts

---

[4] Charles W. Colson, *How Now Shall We Live?* Tyndale Press, Carol Stream, IL, 1999, p. 317.

[5] Ibid., p. 318.

[6] Ibid.

many years. Even as young adults, they are nearly twice as likely to require psychological help. Children from disrupted families have more academic and behavioral problems at school and are nearly twice as likely to drop out of high school. Girls in single-parent homes are at much greater risk for precocious sexuality and are three times more likely to have a child out of wedlock.

Crime and substance abuse are strongly linked to fatherless households. Studies show that 60 percent of rapists grew up in fatherless homes, as did 72 percent of adolescent murderers and 70 percent of all long-term prison inmates. In fact, most of the social pathologies disrupting American life today can be traced to fatherlessness.

Surprisingly, when divorced parents marry again, their children are not any better off, and some studies actually show that children develop increased pathologies. Preschool children in stepfamilies, for example, are forty times more likely to suffer physical or sexual abuse.

Adults are also profoundly harmed by divorce. A study that examined the impact of divorce ten years after the divorce indicated that among two-thirds of divorced couples, one partner is still depressed and financially precarious. And among a quarter of all divorced couples, both former partners are worse off, suffering loneliness and depression.

Divorce affects even physical health. Children of divorce are more prone to illness, accidents, and suicide. Divorced men are twice as likely as married men to die from heart disease, stroke, hypertension, and cancer. They are four times more likely to die in auto accidents and suicide, and their odds are seven times higher for pneumonia and cirrhosis of the liver. Divorced women lose 50 percent more time to illness and injury each year than do married women, and they are two to three times as likely to die of all forms of cancer. Both divorced men and women are almost five times more likely to succumb to substance abuse.

And the effects don't stop with families directly involved. When family breakdown becomes widespread, entire neighborhoods decay. Neighborhoods without fathers are often infected with crime and delinquency. They are often places where teachers cannot teach because misbehaving children disrupt classrooms. Moreover, children of divorce are much more likely to get divorced themselves as adults, so that the negative consequences pass on to the next generation. In this way, family breakdown affects the entire society.

"The impact of divorce on health," says David Larson, president of the National Institute for Healthcare Research, "is like starting to smoke a pack of cigarettes a day."[7]

These statistics may cause some to count their blessings because they have never experienced this familial breakdown. Others may recognize their own family or

---

[7] Charles W. Colson, *How Now Shall We Live?* Tyndale Press, Carol Stream, IL, 1999, p. 232, 234.

extended family in this picture and be discouraged or even bitter that their hopes and dreams have been shattered. Still others may be aware of so many families in this condition that they may have become calloused, assuming this is the norm—a fact of life. Regardless of your own family's experience, there is no doubt that the state of the family in today's society desperately demands our prayer for God's restoration. And what better way to do so than by praying together with our own families?

> **Charles Colson in *How Now Shall We Live?* tells us, "This systematic deconstruction of the oldest, most basic social institution is a prime cause of the social chaos in America in recent decades."**

Interceding For and With Your Family provides an overview of God's design for the family and gives exercises to determine the present state of your own household. It will help you develop a plan to turn your home into a sanctuary, a spiritual outpost for ministry—from which you can then wisely intercede and ask God to help make your home what He desires, *"a house of prayer for all nations"*[8].

The purpose of this book is to increase your joy and the joy of those in your household by helping you invest fifteen minutes daily in kingdom-focused prayer, interceding *for* and *with* your family, and then encouraging you to multiply after your kind, that is, to develop others who will pray for

---

[8] Isaiah 56:7

and with their families. Our joy increases as we conform our lives to the will of God. Families become more joyful as they move toward God's design for them, and relationships in the household are strengthened. If you are one whose family sounds more like the ones described by the quotes at the beginning of this chapter than one representing God's design for families in the Scriptures, let me remind you of our gracious God's ability to *"restore to you the years that the locust hath eaten."*[9] *"Jesus Christ is the same yesterday, today, and forever;"*[10] therefore, He is the One who can overrule the sin of all your yesterdays, give grace for today, and offer bright hope for forever. Let me give you an example.

Regardless of your own family's experience, there is no doubt that the state of the family in today's society desperately demands our prayer for God's restoration. And what better way to do so than by praying together with our own families?

Grace Abounding

Where sin abounded, grace abounded much more.[11]

When Mettie left her home in Silana, Kansas, and entered Peniel College in Bethany, Oklahoma, she planned to

---

[9] Joel 2:25 KJV

[10] Hebrews 13:8

[11] Romans 5:20

become a missionary to Africa. Toward the end of her freshman year, she met J. D., a hardworking, ambitious young man from a strict Christian family. It was not long before J. D. proposed marriage. Mettie wrestled with her attraction to J. D. and her conviction that God wanted her on the mission field. J. D. suggested a solution; if she still felt called to the mission field after they married, he would go with her.

And so they were married. Before Mettie finished her sophomore year, she gave birth to their first son. J. D. was no longer interested in talking about the mission field and Mettie found herself plagued with an ever-present sense of guilt. J. D. worked hard to provide for his growing family, but Mettie never let him forget his broken promise. During the next twenty years, the family grew to a total of eight children. There was almost constant conflict in the home. One sister was killed in an automobile accident, which especially devastated Mettie. J. D. spent more and more time in his business and spent less and less time at home. Then one day, J. D. and Mettie separated; after another ten years, they divorced. J. D. and Mettie were my father and mother. I was their seventh child. One of my early memories, when I was ten years old, was the argument between my parents that finished their marriage forever.

At this same time, my two older brothers joined the army to fight in World War II. My oldest sister was able to fend for herself but this still left my mother to raise three of my sisters and me without any financial help from my father. Over the next five years, I grew so rebellious I was finally sent to live with my father and my new stepmother in Birmingham, Alabama. I resented the fact that, after years of his absence, he now tried to strictly direct every detail of my life. On a cold December night, I slipped out of the house and hitchhiked from Birmingham to Oklahoma City. There I joined the Navy for a four-year tour of duty, which included active combat as a medical corpsman with the 1st Marine Division in Korea.

One year after I was discharged, Christ quickened my heart. I had come to a point of complete desperation when I met a young lady who, realizing I was not a Christian, introduced me to her friend Tom. After Tom shared the Gospel with me, I received Christ as my Savior.

Even though I now had new life in Christ, I determined that marriage was not for me. I told the Lord I would be a celibate monk for life. I was told that the book of Proverbs was the young man's book, so I devoured it. Its many warnings about immoral women reinforced my decision to remain single.[12] But one day as I was reading, I found these words, *"A false balance is abomination to the LORD: but a just weight is His delight."*[13] And God impressed on me that I was out of balance in my thinking on marriage. As I continued to read, I found this Proverb, *"He who finds a wife finds a good thing, and obtains favor from the LORD."*[14] I wanted the Lord's favor so I prayed, "Father, You made Eve for Adam, show me the woman You have made for me."

I entered Bible College in January. Through applying biblical principles to a series of circumstances, I was convinced that Jean was the one God wanted me to marry.

---

[12] See KJV Proverbs 2:16; 5:3; 5:20; 6:24; 7:5; 20:16; 22:14; 23:27; 23:33; 27:13

[13] Proverbs 11:1 KJV

[14] Proverbs 18:22

She was a fellow student in Southeastern Bible College. In April I bought her an engagement ring, and told the Lord that if He gave me the opportunity, I would tell her the "good news." He gave me the opportunity but I chickened out. I returned to my dorm room and tried to read my Bible but the pages might as well have been blank. I knew in my heart that until I did what I told the Lord I would do He would not lead me further. I phoned Jean at her dorm. When she answered I said, "There is something I was supposed to tell you when we were together. I believe the Lord wants us to be husband and wife." For the longest time, she was absolutely silent. Then she said, "Archie, I'm engaged to be married in June to my high school sweetheart." For some reason this did not shake my confidence. With no tact at all I said "Don't make this hard on yourself. If God has to, He will stop you at the altar."

Jean left college in May, expecting to marry in June. For four months I did not see or hear from her, but I prayed. Each time I ate a meal, I asked the Lord to work in Jean's heart and in our circumstances, to bring to pass His will in our lives. In September, Jean returned to college and she was still single! Jean did not know anything about the ring I had purchased the previous April. In December, I asked the Lord for an appropriate situation to place the engagement ring on her finger. He gave the opportunity. I placed the ring on her finger and asked her to marry me. She did not say yes nor did she say no, but she did not take the ring off. We became officially engaged. Then we prayerfully formed a list of needs for the wedding and for starting our life together. The following July 10th, we were married. When we checked our prayer list, we found that God had supplied everything we had asked for.

Our practice of prayer during our engagement continued into a daily practice in marriage. As our three children were conceived, we prayed for them; when they were born we included them in our family worship. This year we celebrated forty-six years together. Each of our three children is now married and we have four grandchildren. Jean and I still pray for and with each other at each meal—even when we are not together—and we also pray at each meal by name for each of our children, their spouses and their children. There have been numerous challenges during our forty-six years of marriage, but even when I have been faithless, our prayer-hearing God has remained faithful.[15]

Sin fractured my parents' lives, devastated their marriage, and devastated my childhood and that of my brothers and sisters. But God has graciously given me a family that is beyond my wildest imaginations. Paul said, *"Where sin abounded, grace abounded much more."*[16]

Prayer is one means God provides for His children to receive His grace, as we pray for and with them. The Lord has promised, *"You will call upon Me and go and pray to Me, and I will listen to you. And you will seek Me and find Me, when you search for Me with all your heart."*[17]

Begin now, through prayer, to increase the flow of God's grace to yourself and your household. *"The LORD is near to all who call upon Him, to all who call upon Him in*

---

[15] See Psalm 65:2 and 2 Timothy 2:13.

[16] Romans 5:20

[17] Jeremiah 29:12-13

truth."[18] "*Seek the* LORD *while He may be found, call upon Him while He is near.*"[19]

Prayer is one means God provides for His children to receive His grace, as we pray for and with them. Begin now, through prayer, to increase the flow of God's grace to yourself and your household.

•••••

---

[18] Psalm 145:18
[19] Isaiah 55:6

God's Design for the Family

In *Improve Your Prayer Life*, we studied a warfare model that provided a framework for learning about the importance of, and approach to, our prayer life. We learned that, "In Israel, men served in the army not only as citizens of the nation, but also as sons of a family, members of a tribe. The army protected the family and the family gave purpose to being in the army."[20] In this book, we are going explore God's design for the family and how to discover and achieve God's purpose for your family through kingdom-focused prayer.

Origin of the Family

The family was first established in Eden while the human race was still in the state of innocence. *"The LORD God said, 'It is not good that man should be alone; I will make him a helper comparable to him.' ...Therefore a man shall leave his father and mother and be joined to his wife, and they shall become one flesh."*[21]

By creating human beings as male and female, He established the interrelatedness of human sexuality, the

---

[20] Archie Parrish, *Improve Your Prayer Life,* Serve International, Atlanta, GA, 2000, p. 38.
[21] Genesis 2:18, 24

25

marital relationship, and the institution of the family, each with its own divinely given moral norms.[22] As husband and wife come together, they form a family, the core institution of human society—the training ground, in fact, for all other social institutions.[23] Through Adam and Eve, the whole human race was propagated.

The family was first established in Eden while the human race was still in the state of innocence.

The Family as the Foundation

God sets the solitary in families.[24]

The family is the nursery, the training school for all institutions of society.[25]

As the human race multiplied, God providentially formed civil governments and ecclesiastical assemblies. These associations allowed for liberty, ownership of property, and public corporate worship. The breakdown of these associations is turning many Americans into savages that roam at large, destitute of faith, insensible of human compassion, and having total disregard for any other's welfare. As long as these associations remain in tact, civil

---

[22] Charles W. Colson, *How Now Shall We Live?* Tyndale Press, Carol Stream, IL, 1999, p. 319.

[23] Ibid., p. 325.

[24] Psalm 68:6

[25] Colson, *How Now Shall We Live?* p. 317

and religious societies continue in the world, and we enjoy their many advantages. But, all civil and religious societies presuppose families. In fact, states and churches are formed out of individuals raised by families.

As the human race multiplied, God providentially formed civil governments and ecclesiastical assemblies. States and churches are formed out of individuals raised by families.

Children are not born pure and innocent, they have an inherent sin nature. Paul explains that Adam's sin brought guilt and corruption on all his descendants.[26] Families have the ministry of turning the raw material of children, *"brought forth in iniquity"*[27] into vital citizens of states and members of churches. The spiritual goal of the family is to produce sons and daughters in God's eternal family, subjects in God's kingdom, soldiers in *Jehovah Tsabaoth's* army. Nothing is more important to civil society and true religion than families following God's divine design, but without prayer for and with our families, doing this is impossible.

God's Purpose for the Family

God clearly expresses His purpose for families through the prophet Malachi:

---

[26] *"Just as through one man sin entered the world, and death through sin, and thus death spread to all men, because all sinned."* Romans 5:12. See also Psalm 51:5.

[27] Psalm 51:5

The LORD has been witness between you and the wife of your youth, with whom you have dealt treacherously; yet she is your companion and your wife by covenant. But did He not make them one, having a remnant of the Spirit? And why one? He seeks godly offspring. Therefore take heed to your spirit, and let none deal treacherously with the wife of his youth. "For the LORD God of Israel says that He hates divorce, for it covers one's garment with violence," says the LORD of hosts. "Therefore take heed to your spirit, that you do not deal treacherously."[28]

The marriage of one man and one woman is the foundation of families. God made one man and one woman, that there might be one of each sex, and that the very creation of human nature might indicate that homosexual and polygamous relations were unnatural. Why did God make but one of each sex when He could have made more? His design was that His people might produce *"godly offspring"*; that is, that husbands and wives might not just give birth to children but that they would *"bring them up in the training and admonition of the Lord."*[29] Therefore, the worship of God must be a consistent part of family life. Engaged couples and newlyweds need to worship together so that they are strong in their own faith and can convey it to their children when God gives them. Then each generation can do the same with the next generation.

Producing godly offspring is not the only goal of the institution of marriage, but Scripture makes it very clear

---

[28] Malachi 2:14-16

[29] Ephesians 6:4

that it is the <u>main</u> goal of marriage. Godly offspring (literally *"a seed of God"*) are children that consciously depend on grace alone to overcome sin's impact in them and to conform them to the likeness of Christ. They, in joyful dependence on God's grace, serve God and are devoted to His glory and honor. And their dependence is expressed in prayer. Family prayer and worship is the God-preferred means for developing godly offspring.

God creates our families not only for this world, but also as a means of preparing all of us for the world to come. God does not bring a man and woman together as husband and wife without an eternal purpose; nor does He place children in families without any thought to their future state. Furthermore, God uses His spiritual family, the Church, to strengthen physical families, and He uses physical families to reinforce His spiritual family, the Church. As the spiritual life of families goes, so goes the spiritual life of the Church and visa versa. If someone believes that our families were formed for this world only, we should ask, "For what was this world made?" Is it our final home? No, this world is a stage through which we pass into our everlasting destination. Our families should be nurseries for heaven. They cannot be if we eliminate devotion to God from them. Therefore, family worship must be cultivated and maintained in our families.

A home where family worship is ignored is barren soil for the nurture of *"godly offspring."* With God, all things are possible, but when family worship is ignored, children, who depend on parents, are denied the greatest advantage they can enjoy as members of a family—learning to love their Creator and to love others. Should prayerless parents expect to have praying children? If we neglect to instruct them in prayer, we cannot expect they will *"grow in the grace and knowledge of our Lord and Savior Jesus Christ.* "[30] Our children see us receive daily mercies from the God of heaven. The Apostle James tells us, *"Every good gift and every perfect gift is from above, and comes down from the Father of lights, with whom there is no variation or shadow of turning."*[31] If we refuse Him the tribute of praise in front of our children, they will probably imitate our ingratitude. They too may go through life ignorant of their obligations to their divine Benefactor.

God creates our families not only for this world, but also as a means of preparing all of us for the world to come. Therefore, family worship must be cultivated and maintained in our families.

Some may say that one's religious faith is a *private* matter and therefore they do not flaunt their faith before their children. One's faith is <u>personal</u> but it cannot be kept <u>private</u>! Faith starts in the privacy of the heart, but if it stays there, it probably never existed in the first place. All believers are to be witnesses[32], to publicly proclaim that Jesus is their Lord. This implies that parents have a special responsibility to pray for and with their children.

As we'll see later in ***Impact Your World***[33], the Bible teaches that God desires the salvation of whole families. Consider these examples.

---

[30] 2 Peter 3:18

[31] James 1:17

[32] See Acts 1:8.

[33] The fourth book of the Kingdom Campaign series.

- A Passover lamb was commanded for each household.[34]

- The Lord commanded Noah to take his whole family into the ark and saved them from the flood.[35]

- God promised to bless all the families of the earth through Abraham.[36]

- The Gadarene demoniac was told to *"Go home to your family and tell them how much the Lord has done for you, and how he has had mercy on you."*[37]

- The Philippian jailer was promised, *"Believe in the Lord Jesus, and you will be saved—you and your household."*[38]

- Crispus, the synagogue ruler, and his entire household believed in the Lord.[39]

- Cornelius, the Roman Centurion, *"called together his relatives and close friends"* to listen to the Gospel from Peter.[40]

- Timothy's faith first lived in his grandmother Lois and in his mother Eunice.[41]

---

[34] Exodus 12:3
[35] Genesis 7:1
[36] Genesis 12:3
[37] Mark 5:19 NIV
[38] Acts 16:31 NIV
[39] Acts 18:8
[40] Acts 10:24
[41] 2 Timothy 1:5

- The first thing Andrew did when he discovered Jesus to be the Messiah was to find his brother Simon and bring him to Jesus.[42]

- Lydia and the members of her household were baptized.[43]

Jonah declares, *"Salvation is of the LORD."*[44] Only the Lord can save anyone. However, in the work of redemption, God makes His people His coworkers in communicating the gospel to all who do not know Him. The fact that parents are believers does not guarantee that their children will be saved. Ultimately each individual is responsible to God for his or her own response to the gospel. But believers are responsible to God, and to those individuals who God, by divine providence, brings into their lives to hear the gospel proclaimed, and to see it lived out in front of them. This is nowhere more apparent than in the role of parents with their children. Believing parents are the primary means appointed by God for the evangelization and nurture of their children.

Having said this, who do you think are more likely to produce *"godly offspring"*? Parents who give no thought to how they will achieve this important responsibility, or parents who make it their main purpose in life to secure God's favor and to prepare for eternity, who daily worship God with their children, and seek His blessing for them. The immortal souls of our children are entrusted to our care. We must give a solemn account of this trust. We cannot think we have faithfully discharged our

---

[42] John 1:40-42

[43] Acts 16:15

[44] Jonah 2:9

32

responsibility while we neglect to maintain our faith in front of our families. If we do, we may be accomplices to their perdition! The blood of our own children may be on our hands!

Jesus said, *"Whoever causes one of these little ones who believe in Me to stumble, it would be better for him if a millstone were hung around his neck, and he were thrown into the sea."*[45] Do we love our children and want the blessing of heaven upon our families? Do we want our children to make their future homes *"houses of prayer"?*[46] Do we want to experience the joy of being God's coworkers in populating heaven and seeing the Christian faith survive and thrive from age to age? Then we must begin the worship of God in our families today and continue until the close of our lives.

God's Order for the Family

God tells us to do all things in an orderly manner.[47] When families comply with God's order for them, they are able to function effectively. Each member of the family is important and compliments the others. God's order in the family does not imply that one role is superior to another. Paul says, *"But I want you to know that the head of every man is Christ, the head of woman is man, and the head of Christ is God."*[48] As the Son and the Father are equal members in the Godhead, so in marriage, husbands and

---

[45] Mark 9:42

[46] See Mark 11:17.

[47] See 1 Corinthians 14:40.

[48] 1 Corinthians 11:3

33

wives are equal, both being members of the "one" they are joined into when they are married. They are *"heirs together of the grace of life."*[49] But just as the members of the Godhead have distinct roles, so in marriage, husbands and wives have distinct roles. These roles provide order within marriage, thereby making possible the smooth and effective functioning of the family unit.

God tells us to do all things in an orderly manner. When families comply with God's order for them, they are able to function effectively. Each member of the family is important and compliments the others. God's order in the family does not imply that one role is superior to another.

Compliance with God's order for families requires leaders to lead and followers to follow. The heads of families are obliged to rule and to provide, not only to exercise authority over those who are dependent upon them, but also to adequately provide the necessities of life for them. Actually, their right to rule is the power to provide for themselves and their dependents. Paul implies this when he says, *"But if anyone does not provide for his own, and especially for those of his household, he has denied the faith and is worse than an unbeliever."*[50]

The Apostle makes failure to *"provide for his own"* totally inconsistent with Christianity. Since the Christian faith is

---

[49] 1 Peter 3:7

[50] 1 Timothy 5:8

both a system of belief and a rule for life, there is an observable unity of belief and action; faith and love are inseparable. To "deny the faith" does not mean apostasy, which is an open denial of the truth of the Christian faith. Rather, here we are dealing with behavior that is a blatant contradiction of one's professed belief. In not showing love, professing Christians demonstrate practically that they are not under the influence of the faith. All the better ancient heathen writers commanded taking care of one's family, and called neglect of one's family unnatural selfishness. So, a professing believer who does not provide for his family is worse than a pagan.

Some use this command to provide for their families to justify their obsessive pursuit of material things. Solomon, the wisest man who ever lived, said, *"If a man tried to buy love with everything he owned, his offer would be utterly despised."*[51] In providing for one's family, there must be a balance of provision for both material and spiritual necessities. Wives and children are not livestock or pets that need only to be fed and watered. Rather, they were made for eternity, endowed with immortal souls. Therefore, the husband's greatest concern for them must be to deal with the eternal world.

There is even more reason for parents to take greater care of their children's immortal spirits than of their perishing bodies. Their comfort in eternity is infinitely more important than their comfort in time. What then shall be said of us if we neglect the souls of those in our care? What shall be said of us if we exert no effort to shape our families for heavenly immortality?

---

[51] Song of Solomon 8:7 NLT

Remember, the truth presented in this book is essential for all people, regardless of their present familial situation. So as you continue to read this book, pray for yourself and the members of both your physical and your spiritual family.

•••••

Our God-given Responsibilities

We have now established God's design for the family; let us continue by studying how praying for and with your family with kingdom focus will enable you to achieve God's purpose for your family. In order to do that, let's consider more specifically what the Bible says are the key roles and duties for each family member. Some of these are specific to our gender or position, but most all are applicable to each of us as bearers of the name of our Savior.

Responsibilities of Both Husbands and Wives

Paul summarizes the responsibilities belonging to both husbands and wives. *"Nevertheless let each one of you in particular so love his own wife as himself, and let the wife see that she respects her husband."*[52] The word, "nevertheless," here is a transition from the spiritual reality of Christ's relationship to the Church. It means that, in spite of Christ's relationship to the Church being an ideal we cannot attain, we should strive to come as close to this ideal in our relationship with our spouse as possible. Having said this, I must acknowledge that explaining marital duties is much easier than doing them! We must

---

[52] Ephesians 5:33

take Ephesians 5:33 to heart and ask God to conform our wills to Scripture.

> **In spite of Christ's relationship to the Church being an ideal we cannot attain, we should strive to come as close to this ideal in our relationship with our spouse as possible.**

In this verse, Paul distills marital duties down to two; to the men, he says every husband's duty is to love his wife. This is not the only duty but it includes all others. He should love her as he loves himself. Here we see both how and why he is to love her—he is to use the "golden rule." Loving her will result in blessings to him—the two of them are one.

Earlier in his letter to the Ephesians, the Apostle says, *"Husbands, love your wives, just as Christ also loved the church and gave Himself for her."*[53] Husbands should live in the presence of their wives as Christ does before His Church. When husbands behave themselves like biblical husbands, they will not be just husbands, they will be ministers of God to their wives—proclaiming to her the love of Christ for the Church, His Bride.

"The husband is head of the wife, as also Christ is head of the church; and He is the Savior of the body."[54] Men are to lead through sacrificial servanthood, giving up their lives to present their wives spotless before the throne, i.e., leading

---

[53] Ephesians 5:25
[54] Ephesians 5:23

in loving humility, which enables their wives to grow in willing submission. The only way this can be accomplished is through family worship. Ignoring this responsibility places us in direct opposition to God's design for marriage.

Another of God's fundamental purposes for marriage is to portray Christ's love for His Church to the watching world, by every couple that believes in Him through grace. If a husband acts indiscreetly towards his wife, if he behaves contrary to Christ, he not only causes his wife to lose the benefit of this ministry, but diminishes the beauty of this relationship, portraying an un-Christ-like picture to the world. For even though a wife can continue to love her husband faithfully when he does not portray Christ, the marriage cannot portray Christ and His Church since Christ is never unfaithful to His Bride.

To the women, Paul in Ephesians 5:33 says it is every wife's duty to respect her husband, both as a person and for his position as her husband. This necessarily includes love, because if she loves him, she will admire and esteem him, she will show consideration for him and try to please him. Even when a wife appears to be the sweetest thing on earth and her husband the meanest man alive, she still has the responsibility to respect him. Scripture says husbands are more likely to change for the good if their wives respect them properly. Peter urges, *"Wives, likewise, be submissive to your own husbands, that even if some do not obey the word, they, without a word, may be won by the conduct of their wives, when they observe your chaste conduct accompanied by fear."*[55] Likewise, many wives

---

[55] 1 Peter 3:1-2

can be won to respect by her husband's affection and wisdom.

A godly wife's respect is a picture of the ideal submission of the Church to Christ. Listen to the Apostle Paul address this: *"Just as the church is subject to Christ, so let the wives be to their own husbands in everything."*[56] It is important to point out that if a husband urges his wife to do what God forbids, or prohibits his wife to do what God requires, she should refuse submission. The wife is bound in conscience to obey her husband in everything that is not contrary to the revealed will of God, and even in that case, she should refuse respectfully. In this way, the wife should honor her husband, second only to God. If she really respects him, it will show in what she says about him to others, *"On her tongue is the law of kindness."*[57] Thus, she should always strive for *"a gentle and quiet spirit."*[58]

Again, just as the husband's love for his wife is difficult to attain in light of the standard—Christ's love for the Church—a wife's godly submission is not an easy or natural task. But remember, this is our Creator's counsel, clearly articulated in both the Old and New Testaments, by both Paul the Apostle to the Gentiles[59] and Peter the Apostle to the Jews.[60] These two duties (husband—love, wife—respect) are not exhaustive, but are mentioned particularly because they include all other duties and are the most common failures of each. Paul emphasizes that

---

[56] Ephesians 5:24

[57] Proverbs 31:26 See also Proverbs 15:4.

[58] 1 Peter 3:4

[59] See Ephesians 5:23 ff. and Colossians 3:18.

[60] See 1 Peter 3:1 ff.

respect is what husbands need most from their wives, and love is what wives need most from their husbands. A godly marriage with mutual love and respect is a bit of heaven on earth. Reflecting on these duties should humble all of us for our past failures and challenge us to future improvement.

The husband's love and the wife's respect are the foundation for eleven duties shared by both:

- *Living with each other*
- *Loving each other*
- *Staying faithful to each other*
- *Helping each other*
- *Being patient with each other*
- *Encouraging each other to trust Christ as Savior*
- *Maintaining intimacy*
- *Looking out for each other's interests in all things*
- *Praying for each other*
- *Seeking and obeying God*
- *Keeping ungodly materials out of the house*

Living with Each Other

A husband must *"leave his father and mother and be joined to his wife."*[61] He must dwell with his wife.[62] Any husband who defies this truth lives in the willful neglect of the explicit will of God, and his family may become a nursery for hell. A wife is to *"forget your own people also, and your father's house."*[63] The wife must not *"depart*

---

[61] Genesis 2:24

[62] See 1 Peter 3:7.

[63] Psalm 45:10

from her husband,"[64] even if he is an unbeliever. All other duties of marriage presuppose living together. The Old Testament prohibits husbands from going to war during their first year of marriage,[65] showing the importance of living together.

Loving Each Other

To love each other is both the husband's[66] and the wife's[67] duty. Love is the great reason and comfort of marriage—not merely romantic love but genuine and constant affection that cares for each other *"fervently with a pure heart."*[68] Marital love cannot be based on beauty or wealth, for these pass away. Marital love cannot be based even on piety, for that may decay. It must be based on God's commands because they never change. The marriage vow obligates "for better or for worse." Married persons are to consider their own spouses the best person in the world for them. Their love for each other must endure through the ups and downs—the celebrations and the challenges. This truehearted love produces true contentment and comfort. It guards against jealousy and adultery. It decreases family conflict. Without it, the marriage is like a bone out of joint. There is pain until it is restored.

---

[64] 1 Corinthians 7:10

[65] See Deuteronomy 24:5.

[66] See Colossians 3:19.

[67] See Titus 2:4.

[68] 1 Peter 1:22

Staying Faithful to Each Other

Every husband should *"have* (sexually) *his own wife,"* and every wife her own husband.[69] Husbands should imitate the first Adam, who had but one wife, and the second Adam, who has but one Church. The marriage covenant binds us to our own spouse as the dearest, sweetest and best in the world. The slightest infidelity, even in the heart, may lead to full-blown adultery. Without repentance, adultery, like any sin, destroys both earthly happiness and reasonable assurance of heaven.[70] It has the potential to dissolve marriages. In the Old Testament, adultery was a capital crime[71] because it desecrated the means God provided to procreate creatures who were His image bearers. We must be extremely careful to avoid all temptations to this sin. The man or woman who is not satisfied with one mate will never be satisfied with many. This sin has no boundaries!

Women, as a rule, tend to be more open and share intimate things more readily. Men are usually slow to share. This makes them more vulnerable in the area of sexual morality. Patrick Morley gives suggests a man make himself accountable to another man in regard to several questions:
- How has God blessed you this week? (What went right?)
- What problem has consumed your thoughts this week? (What went wrong?)
- Have you read God's Word daily? (How long? Why not? Will you next week?)

---

[69] 1 Corinthians 7:2

[70] See 1 Corinthians 6:9-10, Galatians 5:19-21, Hebrews 13:4 and Revelation 21:8.

[71] See Deuteronomy 22:22.

- Describe your prayers. (For yourself, for others, praise, confession, gratitude)
- How is your relationship with Christ changing?
- How have you been tempted this week? How did you respond?
- Do you have any unconfessed sin in your life?
- Are you walking in the Spirit?
- Did you worship in church this week? (Was your faith in Jesus strengthened? Was He honored?)
- Have you shared your faith? In what ways? How can you improve?
- How is it going with your wife? (Attitudes, time, irritations, disappointments, progress, her relationship with Christ)
- How is it going with the kids? (Quantity and quality of time, values and beliefs, education, spiritual welfare)
- How are your finances doing? (Debts, sharing, saving, stewardship)
- How are things going on the job? (career progress, relationships, temptations, work load, stress, problems, working too much)
- Do you feel in the center of God's will? Do you sense His peace?
- What are you wrestling with in your thought life?
- What have you done for someone else this week? (The poor, encouragement, service)
- Are your priorities in the right order?
- Is your moral and ethical behavior what it should be?
- How are you doing in your personal high-risk area?
- Is the "visible" you and the "real" you consistent in this relationship?[72]

---

[72] Patrick Morley, *The Man in the Mirror,* Thomas Nelson Publishers, Nashville, TN, 1992, p. 287-288

These questions provide excellent opportunity for introspection in an individual's prayers for the family. In addition, it might be good to adapt some of the questions and include them in corporate worship with the family. However, be wise in the way you use these questions in family worship. Young children should not be drawn into matters that are beyond their ability to handle.

Faithfulness also involves keeping each other's secrets. These must not be disclosed unless there is a greater moral obligation. Telling your spouse's secrets is a bad thing to do when done accidentally, worse when done as the result of temper or bad judgment, and worst when motivated by hate.

Helping Each Other

Scripture says the wife should be *"a helper comparable"*[73] to her husband, implying that a husband and wife should help each other. For motivation, let him give attention to the entire book of Proverbs, and her to the last chapter especially. Many newlyweds expect only happiness in marriage, but trouble is bound to come.[74] A couple may face loss of worldly goods, harm to their children, and afflictions from both friends and enemies. But, spouses must be friends to each other through thick and thin—soul friends, laughing and weeping together, with nothing but death separating them. They may have separate interests, but should have some in common as well. They should live as *"heirs together of the grace of life."*[75]

---

[73] Genesis 2:18

[74] See 1 Corinthians 7:28 NIV.

[75] 1 Peter 3:7

The highest end of marriage is to promote the family's eternal joy. Cooperation here is very important. When the husband is home, he must instruct and pray with his family and sanctify the Sabbath, but in his absence, the wife must do these things. Also, when the husband is an unbeliever or unwilling to assume this responsibility, the wife should winsomely do so. Timothy's father was a Gentile who appears not to have contributed to Timothy's spiritual development. In spite of this, Paul said to Timothy, *"from childhood you have known the Holy Scriptures."*[76] Paul also called *"to remembrance the genuine faith"* which was in Timothy, and added that this *"genuine faith ...dwelt first in your grandmother Lois and your mother Eunice."*[77]

Being Patient with Each Other

We owe patience to all,[78] but especially to our spouse. There are many temptations in marriage to become impatient! Hot tempers ignite civil wars and no good ever comes of them. Both husband and wife need to cultivate a meek and quiet spirit. We must learn to hold our criticisms, to use care and wisdom in working through conflicts, and to make good use of "cooling off" periods. This does not mean that we should run from disagreements or fail to communicate about unpleasant things; it means we must learn to disagree without being disagreeable, being careful not to lose our tempers. Ask God for grace and wisdom to avoid potential storms. We must, when we marry, remember that we are not perfect people, but two sinful children of Adam who together will assist with each

---

[76] 2 Timothy 3:15

[77] 2 Timothy 1:3-5

[78] 1 Thessalonians 5:14

other's mutual sanctification. "Wink" (be generously forgiving) at lesser faults, and be careful in confronting greater ones. The Bible tells us we must acknowledge our faults to one another[79] and confess them all to God[80]; we are to yield to one another rather than to the devil.[81]

Each should inquire into the other's spiritual state, using the God-appointed means to help each other improve. John Chrysostom, Archbishop of Constantinople in 407 A.D., said, "Let them both go to church, then discuss the sermon together." If both are Christians already, then they should do what they can to help each other to become mature saints. We should speak often of God and spiritual things. We are fellow-pilgrims on our way to the Celestial City.[82]

Encouraging Each Other to Trust Christ as Savior

Although Paul lived by the principle that he became *"all things to all men,"* that he *"might by all means save some,"*[83] believers are not to enter knowingly into marriage

---

[79] James 5:16 KJV

[80] 1 John 1:9

[81] See Ephesians 4:27.

[82] See *The Pilgrim's Progress* by John Bunyan, published by Moody Press, Chicago.

[83] 1 Corinthians 9:22 Scripture is abundantly clear that only God can save anyone, but it is also clear that God usually uses the prayerful proclamation of the gospel to save sinners. James tells us *"he who turns a sinner from the error of his way will save a soul from death and cover a multitude of sins."* (James 5:20) Jude tells us we are to save others *"with fear, pulling them out of the fire."* (Jude 1:23) And, to Timothy, Paul exhorted, *"Take heed to yourself and to the doctrine. Continue in them, for in doing this you will save both yourself and those who hear you."* (1 Timothy 4:16)

with unbelievers.[84]   Today many believers, through ignorance or disregard of this truth are married to unbelievers. When Christians discover themselves in this situation, they are not to leave their mate; their driving passion should be their mate's salvation. Paul indicates that the greatest duty of husbands and wives is to encourage their spouses to trust Christ as Savior.[85] Peter tells us that some unbelieving husbands *"may be won by the conduct of their wives, when they observe your chaste conduct accompanied by fear."*[86] One who loves both Christ and their unbelieving spouse will do everything in their power—they will live, pray, and share the gospel in order to see their mate trust Christ.

Maintaining Intimacy

God designed sex for three purposes: procreation, communication and recreation. To Adam and Eve, God said, *"Be fruitful and multiply; fill the earth and subdue it."*[87] When a man and woman come together sexually and the woman conceives and bears a child, that couple comes as close to godlike creativity as is humanly possible. The Creator designed the human race so that we can be His coworkers in populating the earth and, ultimately, heaven. By divine design, we produce the physical nature of a child, but God alone is the *"the Father of spirits."*[88] God may not be uppermost in a couple's thoughts as they engage in

---

[84] 2 Corinthians 6:14

[85] See 1 Corinthians 7:16.

[86] 1 Peter 3:1-2

[87] Genesis 1:28

[88] Hebrews 12:9

sexual intercourse, but they could never procreate a living child if He were not directly involved in their intimacy.

Science now provides some ability to control birth. Christians' use of birth control is a topic for another book. However, it is safe to say that a large segment of our society today rejects any concept of absolute truth and rebels against all authority; so they reject God from their lives and especially their bedrooms. They do not see sex as a partnership with God for the purpose of procreating "godly offspring" who will be conformed to the likeness of Christ. With God out of the picture, the highest view of sex is, at best, an act of intimate communication between two people who love one another. For many people however, sex is nothing more than recreation or sport. It can be participated in alone, or with various members of the opposite sex or even of the same gender.

The Bible declares, *"Marriage is honorable among all, and the bed undefiled; but fornicators and adulterers God will judge."*[89] Sex is designed to remedy impure affections, not excite them. Within the bounds of marriage, Christians are free to enjoy sexual intimacy. The Song of Solomon is rich with sexual expressions for the purposes of communication and recreation between married lovers. But not everything people may desire to do sexually is permissible or wise between married believers. A husband is never free to rape his wife just because he is married to her. Christians cannot follow every sexual folly they can imagine with their spouse, just because they are married, just as owning wine gives you no permission to get drunk. Christians are to be moderate and sensible. For example, we might

---

[89] Hebrews 13:4

49

abstain for a time to give ourselves to prayer.[90] Especially in marital relations, we must show reverence to God and respect for each other. True love does not behave rudely. Those people who have participated in sexual practices before marriage must ask the Lord to sanctify their desires and practices for the marriage bed. Above all, Christians are to seek God's glory in all things, and that includes sex. The old saying is true: "The secular becomes spiritual when the focus of the heart is eternal, and the spiritual becomes secular when the focus of the heart is temporal."

Looking Out for Each Other's Interests in All Things

This means that a husband and wife are to be concerned about each other's health and welfare, empathizing with each other in sickness and in health, at least in spirit. One should not be rich while the other suffers want. For example, a husband should not buy top of the line golf clubs while his wife or children lack food or clothing.

Looking out for each other's interest means we should also promote each other's good reputation. A husband naturally and rightly cares for things that are of the world, as well as how he may please his wife, and the wife does the same for her husband.[91] This way of acting brings honor to their faith, comfort to their lives, and gives them a godly contentment with what they have and with who they are.

---

[90] See 1 Corinthians 7:5.

[91] See 1 Corinthians 7:33-34.

Praying for Each Other

Peter warns us that living together without understanding can hinder receiving God's answer to our prayers.[92]   To live together with understanding suggests that husbands and wives should pray for and with each other. We should pray for everyone God puts on our hearts, but especially for our spouse. *"Isaac pleaded with the LORD for his wife, because she was barren."*[93] Earnest prayer expresses the purest love and preserves it. Therefore husbands and wives must seek times for prayer together. Prayer is one sure way to elevate a Christian marriage above the marriages of non-Christians and to distinguish the relationship from mere cohabitation.

Seeking and Obeying God

Both husbands and wives should seek to obey God without any reservation. When we are born again and are seeking to grow in the grace and knowledge of Christ, we can more aptly please God and be a better mate to our spouse. Without Christ, we can only live together as civil pagans. This is seen in the everyday working out of our faith within the marital relationship. For instance, the husband that truly fears God cannot remain bitter against his wife.[94] Reading the Bible together daily will eliminate many conflicts, comfort many distresses, and guide in many confounding circumstances. Remember, because God's commands have the highest authority, obedience has the greatest sweetness.

---

[92] See 1 Peter 3:7.

[93] Genesis 25:21

[94] See Colossians 3:19.

We should seek to keep the Golden Rule in our marriage, *"Whatever you want men to do to you, do also to them."*[95] Righteousness outside the home will not excuse wickedness at home. When a husband and wife each focus on their own duties to the other, they will be blessed. Marriage is not a 50/50 relationship. Both parties must give 100%, regardless of whether or not the other spouse is "giving." It is not a matter of the husband loving his wife on condition that she loves him back. Our lesson here is how Christ unconditionally loves the Church. *"While we were yet sinners, Christ died for us."*[96] He gave His life (100%), while we not only were giving nothing, but also were hostile to Him (less than 0%).

Both husbands and wives should pray for spiritual graces, especially wisdom, humility, and uprightness. James promises, *"If any of you lacks wisdom, let him ask of God, who gives to all liberally and without reproach, and it will be given to him. But let him ask in faith, with no doubting, for he who doubts is like a wave of the sea driven and tossed by the wind."*[97] A lack of wisdom causes many problems in marriage. We need much wisdom to love as husbands, and to respect as wives.

Humility keeps the husband from becoming a tyrant, and keeps the wife ready to submit. *"By pride comes nothing but strife."*[98] *"God resists the proud, but gives grace to the humble."*[99] *"Humble yourselves in the sight of the Lord,*

---

[95] Matthew 7:12

[96] Romans 5:8 KJV

[97] James 1:5-6

[98] Proverbs 13:10

[99] James 4:6

and He will lift you up. "[100] A proud person is self-centered, and would not agree even with an angel from heaven. Humble husbands and wives will say, "My spouse is far too good for a sinner like me. I don't deserve such a wonderful partner." Truly humble people are pleasant companions. Humility also promotes contentment.

An upright heart will choose the right course, even when it is the hardest. It will endure the worst injury rather than cause the least. It will watch against the beginnings of sin, being careful that sin does not become full-blown and produce the worst troubles in a marriage. Upright husbands and wives will strive each to do their own duty, and will be most severe against their own failures.[101]

Keeping Ungodly Materials Out of the House

Paul warns, *"Do not be deceived: 'Evil company corrupts good habits.'"*[102] Scripture implies that husbands and wives are not to allow any ungodly, profane, or heretical materials in the house. By materials, I mean things that tend to provoke looseness of morals, or things that oppose the basic truths of the gospel. This may include magazines, books, CDs, videos, many TV programs, audiocassettes, immoral Internet web pages, etc. All Christians must allow liberty in things which are not prohibited by Scripture; but all Christians should abstain from anything that strikes either at faith or holiness—their own or their family's.[103]

---

[100] James 4:10

[101] From a sermon by D. Scott Meadows, pastor of Calvary Baptist Church, a Reformed Baptist Congregation in Exeter, New Hampshire.

[102] 1 Corinthians 15:33

[103] See Romans 14.

Peter counsels, *"Dear friends, I urge you, as aliens and strangers in the world, to abstain from sinful desires, which war against your soul."*[104] This is especially important for pastors of churches and heads of families, because should a leader fall, the effect on the followers is devastating. The neglect of this principle has brought ruin in many families and churches. It is easier than we might think to undermine entire households by allowing the deceiver a foothold.[105]

We see Jacob practice this control. He commanded his family and all that were with him to put away the strange gods from among them and to change their garments.[106] In the book of Acts, new Christians also set a good example for us. *"Many of those who had practiced magic brought their books together and burned them in the sight of all. And they counted up the value of them, and it totaled fifty thousand pieces of silver."*[107] That was a lot of money in those days!

Three Roles for Husbands— Prophet, Priest and King

Every husband has three roles: a prophet to instruct; a priest to pray for and with; and a king to lead, govern, direct, and provide for his family. God will require an accounting of how husbands fulfill all three of these roles. We have already discussed how a man is to act in the office of king—providing for and leading his family. Christ the

---

[104] 1 Peter 2:11 NIV

[105] See Titus 1:10-11.

[106] Genesis 35:2

[107] Acts 19:19

King leads His followers in spiritual battle; hence, a man must lead his family in spiritual battle, giving direction and leadership against the attack of the enemy.

Every husband has three roles: a prophet to instruct; a priest to pray for and with; and a king to lead, govern, direct, and provide for his family. Christ the King leads His followers in spiritual battle; hence, a man must lead his family in spiritual battle, giving direction and leadership against the attack of the enemy.

As pastors are obliged to promote the spiritual growth of every individual person under their charge, so, every household is a parish, and all family heads are responsible to secure, as much as they are able, the spiritual prosperity of everyone under their roof. Pastors are to teach people publicly and from house to house.[108] Suppose pastors did not do this, and excused themselves by saying that they had enough to do to work out their own salvation with fear and trembling?[109] What if they had no time to concern themselves with the spiritual life of others? Would you not think such pastors to be like the unjust judge who did not fear God nor regard any man?[110] Horrible as such characters would be, they are no worse than a family head, who thinks himself obliged only to care for his own soul without paying any regard to the souls of his family. Thus,

---

[108] See Acts 20:20.

[109] See Philippians 2:12.

[110] See Luke 18:1-8.

husbands are to fulfill the role of priest by praying for his family. Note well God's words through Malachi:

> *Behold, I will send you Elijah the prophet before the coming of the great and dreadful day of the LORD. And he will turn the hearts of the fathers to the children, and the hearts of the children to their fathers, lest I come and strike the earth with a curse.*[111]

Today, we have the written word of God, and it is a man's duty as head of the household to ensure that this word is learned and applied. God's word provides us with examples of godly fathers whom we should imitate: Job, Abraham, Isaac, Jacob, Joshua.

Job

The book of Job is the oldest existing book in the world. In Job 1:5, Job's regular care over his children is recorded: *"So it was, when the days of feasting had run their course, that Job would send and sanctify them, and he would rise early in the morning and offer burnt offerings according to the number of them all. For Job said, 'It may be that my sons have sinned and cursed God in their hearts.'"*[112]

Abraham

Abraham was "father of the faithful" and the friend of God. For his domestic piety, Jehovah blessed him: *"For I have known him, in order that he may command his children and*

---

[111] Malachi 4:5-6
[112] Job 1:5

his household after him, that they keep the way of the LORD, to do righteousness and justice."[113] God selected Abraham so that he would instruct his children and servants in the most important of all duties—*"the way of the Lord"*—that is, the truth about God's glorious person, His high claim upon us, and what He requires from us. Note well the words *"I have known him, in order that he may command."* God's gave him authority for spiritual leadership as father and head of his house; he was to enforce the duties of family godliness. If a father's leadership in the family flows from his own personal godliness, consistently exemplified, then producing *"godly offspring"* is basically a matter of multiplying after one's kind.[114] As a father and grandfather, I quickly confess that acknowledging my imperfections, errors, and sins is an essential element in realistic godliness.

Prayer was an indispensable part of Abraham's leadership. Wherever he pitched his tent, he *"built an altar to the LORD."*[115] We are *"Abraham's seed,"*[116] therefore, we must do *"the works of Abraham"*[117] and not neglect the weighty duty of family worship.

---

[113] Genesis 18:19

[114] God has built into all creation the principle that living things *"multiply after their kind."* (See Genesis 1:11-12, 21, 24-25 KJV.) Paul indicates multiplication is important in the realm of the spiritual also. To Timothy he said, *"The things that you have heard from me among many witnesses, commit these to faithful men who will be able to teach others also."* (2 Timothy 2:2)

[115] Genesis 12:7 See also Genesis 13:4.

[116] Galatians 3:29

[117] John 8:39

Isaac and Jacob

By the influence of Abraham's good example and instructions, his son and grandson followed the same practice. They too built altars to the Lord wherever they pitched their tents.[118] In those times, altars were necessary for proper worship of God.

Joshua

On the eve of leading Israel to conquer Canaan, Joshua declares to all, *"If it seems evil to you to serve the LORD, choose for yourselves this day whom you will serve, whether the gods which your fathers served that were on the other side of the River, or the gods of the Amorites, in whose land you dwell. But as for me and my house, we will serve the LORD."*[119] Neither his high office nor his pressing public duties were allowed to crowd out his attention to the spiritual well-being of his family.

The Role for Wives—
Sacrificial Love as an Act of Worship

Just as the three-part role for husbands can be challenging, so the role of wives is equally difficult. Susan Hunt states emphatically:

> It is time for women of biblical faith to reclaim our territory. We know the Designer. We have His instruction manual. If we don't display the Divine

---

[118] See Genesis 26:25; 28:18-22; 33:20.
[119] Joshua 24:15

design of His female creation, no one will. But if we do, it will be a profound testimony to a watching, needy world.[120]

A Christian woman, as the completer of her husband, will use her God-given gifts in mercy and nurturing, watching over the affairs of her household,[121] practicing hospitality[122] and doing good deeds "such as bringing up the children, showing hospitality, washing the feet of the saints, helping those in trouble and devoting herself to all kinds of good deeds."[123]

With so many women working outside the home today, whether by necessity or by choice, there is great stress placed on families. There simply is not enough time or energy to go around. Usually, a woman's relationship with her husband is the first to suffer. When this is the case, reverencing a woman's husband may entail looking for ways to work from within the home, or perhaps giving up an outside career until the children are grown. Perhaps it is necessary to make some changes in lifestyle in order to accommodate a woman's ability to stay home to care for her husband and family. Perhaps more than any other, a wife/mother knows the self-sacrifice that is needed in order to fill the biblical mandate—a sacrifice that Christ Himself made in taking our place of punishment and death upon Himself at the cross. Instead of having a dim view of a woman's calling to sacrificial love, it should be seen as a

---

[120] Susan Hunt, *By Design*, Legacy Communications, Franklin, TN 1994, p. 17.

[121] Proverbs 31:27

[122] Romans 12:13

[123] 1 Timothy 5:10

high and holy calling—a duty, a privilege, and a joy—an opportunity to become more like Christ each moment of every day by dying to self and living for others.

Just as being a servant-leader is a sacrificial job for a man, so being a wife and mother is a sacrificial occupation for a woman. Paul tells us that our obedience to God's design and calling on our lives is our spiritual act of worship. Children often learn sacrifice and service, mercy and hospitality from their mothers. They learn to respect, honor and obey their father, as she practices godly submission. And, her husband's completion of his role becomes a joy as she encourages him by her participation in family worship.

> **Just as being a servant-leader is a sacrificial job for a man, so being a wife and mother is a sacrificial occupation for a woman. Paul tells us that our obedience to God's design and calling on our lives is our spiritual act of worship.**

The human sin nature makes it very easy to remind husbands and children of how much a woman has sacrificed. Doing so, especially in an unloving way, leads to a most unhappy home, and greatly confuses children. The natural instinct for them when they grow up is to resist "being a doormat"; occasionally some may conclude that cheerful sacrifice is what is needed instead. A woman who learns and models her biblical role, participating joyfully in family worship, and setting the tone of cheerful obedience to Christ and to her husband, will provide an example for both her male and female children, as well as to the watching world.

Children's Duty--Honor

God puts special emphasis on the role of children in families by making one of the Ten Commandments: *"Honor your father and your mother, that your days may be long upon the land which the LORD your God is giving you."*[124] Children should honor their parents, always counting their parents better than themselves.

At different times in their lives, some children slight and scorn their parents—during teen-age years, after receiving their educational degrees, when the culture and times begin to pass their parents by, or when their parents reach an age where they require their children's care. Solomon warned, *"The eye that mocks his father, and scorns obedience to his mother, the ravens of the valley will pick it out, and the young eagles will eat it."*[125] Children are to show honor to their parents, through obedience, and by a willingness to help them when they have opportunity to see an unfulfilled need. *"If any widow has children or grandchildren, let them first learn to show piety at home and to repay their parents,"* says Paul, for that *"is good and acceptable before God."*[126]

Joseph, though he ruled beside the king in Egypt, observed this principle toward Jacob, his poor father.[127] When Hophni and Phinehas, refused the wise counsel of their

---

[124] Exodus 20:12 See also Leviticus 19:3; Proverbs 15:5; 20:20; 28:24; 30:11; Ephesians 6:1-3; and Colossians 3:20.

[125] Proverbs 30:17

[126] 1 Timothy 5:4

[127] Genesis 41:39-44; 47:12.

father, they provoked God to be their enemy.[128]   God himself hanged Absalom for rebelling against his father,[129] even though David had not been a model father to him.[130]

Children are to show honor to their parents, through obedience, and by a willingness to help them when they have opportunity to see an unfulfilled need.

God takes note of children that grieve their parents. He heard Abraham's groan for Ishmael: *"Oh, that Ishmael might live before You!"*[131]   He observed when Isaac and Rebekah grieved for the misbehavior of Esau.[132]   He listened when David bitterly mourned for his son Absalom, who died in his wickedness.[133] The parable of the prodigal son is perhaps one of the most well-known and well-loved parts of the Bible, and reveals the heart of our waiting heavenly Father to all His children: When children repent of their sin, they will find both their earthly father and their Heavenly Father rejoicing: *"This my son was dead and is*

---

[128] See 1 Samuel 2:23-25.

[129] See 2 Samuel 18:9.

[130] See 2 Samuel 13 and 14. David's failure to deal with his son Amnon's rape of Tamar (his daughter, Absalom's sister and Amnon's half-sister) gave room for Absalom's hatred of Amnon. When Absalom took revenge by killing Amnon, it led to his exile. Again David failed to reconcile this situation until several years had passed, and he had received much prompting from others.

[131] Genesis 17:18

[132] Genesis 26:34-35

[133] 2 Samuel 18:32-33

alive again; he was lost, and is found.' And they began to be merry. "[134]

Parent's Responsibilities to Children— Instruction, Correction and Prayer

The first responsibility of parents is to instruct their children. In reference to the laws of Israel, Moses commanded, *"Teach them diligently to your children,"* and *"talk of them when you sit in your house, when you walk by the way, when you lie down, and when you rise up."*[135] And Paul counsels, *"You, fathers, do not provoke your children to wrath, but bring them up in the training and admonition of the Lord."*[136] And, *"Fathers, do not provoke your children, lest they become discouraged."*[137]

We must prayerfully choose instructors for our children with great care. If we do not wish our children to get burned, we must not put them into the fire. The teachers of our children must be the kind that will help us build Christian character in them. Our children have too long been educated without direct, focused reference to the glory of Christ and to their responsibilities in this fallen world. All Christians are to be *"salt"* and *"light"* in society.[138] Parents must choose the best teachers possible for our children, but we can never relinquish our own responsibility to teach them biblical truth, and to monitor the teaching they receive from all other sources.

---

[134] Luke 15:24

[135] Deuteronomy 6:7

[136] Ephesians 6:4

[137] Colossians 3:21

[138] See Matthew 5:13-16.

Parents also have the duty of correction. Solomon speaks much to this point: *"Correct your son, and he will give you rest; yes, he will give delight to your soul."*[139] Discipline in the early years will mean less correction required in later years.

Instruction and correction must be preceded and followed with prayer to God for our children. The privilege and duty of parents is to train sons and daughters for the service of Christ. But *"who is sufficient for these things?"*[140] God promises, *"My grace is sufficient for you, for my power is made perfect in weakness."*[141] And He urges us to *"come boldly to the throne of grace, that we may obtain mercy and find grace to help in time of need."*[142] All our work as parents should begin at the throne of grace. If we fail to do this, we will fail in all that is important for us to do in raising our children.

---

[139] Proverbs 29:17 Also, *"Foolishness is bound up in the heart of a child; the rod of correction will drive it far from him."* (Proverbs 22:15) *"He who spares his rod hates his son, but he who loves him disciplines him promptly."* (Proverbs 13:24) *"Chasten your son while there is hope, and do not set your heart on his destruction."* (Proverbs 19:18) *"Do not withhold correction from a child, for if you beat him with a rod, he will not die. You shall beat him with a rod, and deliver his soul from hell."* (Proverbs 23:13-14) *"The rod and rebuke give wisdom, but a child left to himself brings shame to his mother."* (Proverbs 29:15) When the Bible refers to beating children, it certainly does not mean to abuse them; it simply says parents are to provide correction in the form of physical spanking—not done in anger, but calmly, privately, and sparingly. When we heed this counsel, our words of reproof to our children will be sober, few, and pertinent.

[140] 2 Corinthians 2:16

[141] 2 Corinthians 12:9 NIV

[142] Hebrews 4:16

We must have wisdom from above if we are to train servants for the Most High. When we talk with God about specific situations relating to each of our children, we will find help which human wisdom could never provide. On the last day, we will see that the secret of successful Christian parenting was prayer. Therefore, we must continue *"steadfastly in prayer."*[143]

By making intercession for and with our children, we can cultivate a sense of parental accountability. God holds parents responsible to provide the means necessary to shape the character of our children. Therefore, parents must teach children the truths of God's word; we must pray for and with our children, and most of all, we must model grace-driven godliness before our children.

We will give account *"in the day of judgment"*[144] for what we do, or neglect to do, to develop our children's characters. May we train them so well that, by God's grace, He will use them for the salvation of hundreds, maybe even thousands. May we not neglect their training, for if we do, our children's blood and the blood of those negatively influenced by them may be on our hands.[145] We cannot avoid this responsibility. What we do with it will meet us in the judgment.

If we are faithful in the prayer closet, and in doing what we there acknowledge to be our duty, we will find sufficient sustaining grace to do what must be done outside the prayer closet. And the thought will be delightful: "I am permitted

---

[143] Romans 12:12

[144] Matthew 12:36

[145] See Ezekiel 33:8.

to train these immortals to glorify God through the salvation of souls."

To properly train our children, we must have a devoted spirit ourselves. Our souls must be healthy and prosperous in the Lord; they must burn with love for Christ and His kingdom. All our instructions must be enforced by a godly example, if we want to lead our children to live devoted lives. A father who raised a large family, most of whom had become committed to Christ, was asked what he did to have his children turn out so well. "I have tried so to live," said he, "as to show them that it was my grand purpose to go to heaven and to take them along with me."

We must pray and work for the early conversion of our children, regarding every day our children live out of Christ as an increase of their danger and guilt. A mother of a large family of committed Christians gave this testimony of how she had led her children to faith: "I felt that if they were not converted before seven or eight years of age, they would probably be lost; and when they approached that age, I agonized in prayer lest they should grow up impenitent. God has not turned away my prayers nor his mercy from me."

Pray! *"Arise, cry out in the night, at the beginning of the watches; pour out your heart like water before the face of the Lord. Lift your hands toward Him for the life of your young children."*[146] Hope for the early provision of divine grace. He has promised, *"For I will pour water on him who is thirsty, and floods on the dry ground; I will pour My Spirit on your descendants, and My blessing on your*

---

[146] Lamentations 2:19

offspring; they will spring up among the grass like willows by the watercourses. One will say, 'I am the LORD's'; another will call himself by the name of Jacob; another will write with his hand, 'The LORD's,' and name himself by the name of Israel. "[147]

The history of many families proves the power of this promise. It is in young hearts that we find the best places in which to lay deep, broad, and strong spiritual foundations. There is no assurance that your child will do anything for Christ till he or she comes to the foot of the cross by faith, repenting, believing, and surrendering.

It is an interesting and important fact that children even under the age of four years have been known to feel deep convictions of sin against God, to sorrow for sin, to believe on Christ, to fix their affections on God, and to show all the evidences of saving grace seen in adults. So, therefore, parents should desire the early conversion of their children, that they may have the longest possible time in this world to serve Christ, as well as the blessing of living their earthly lives without possibly experiencing irreversible consequences of forgiven sin. If our children's childhood is devoted to Christ, their adult years are more likely to be marked with more maturity of Christian character and fitness for more fruitful labors for Christ.

We must pray and work at developing close spiritual relationships with our children. Talk with them freely and lovingly on issues of the Christian faith. Blend Christian intimacy into all your family activities. Then, if your children die at an early age or before you, you will know

---

[147] Isaiah 44:3-5

their spiritual condition and the progress of their preparation *"to depart and be with Christ."*[148]

We must prayerfully keep before our children the great object for which they should live: the glory of God and the salvation of sinners. Teach and demonstrate to your children the importance of placing at the foot of the cross all of their attainments, eminence, influence, honor, and wealth—all things; and to live with one desire, *"Father, glorify Thy name."*[149] Train your children to present the Gospel, and make a habit of including them with you when you witness. Evangelism will become a way of life for them—natural and nothing to be afraid of. Pray with them about people they might have occasion to reach for Christ.

We must do both the essential and the important. Not doing something that is essential, even though we do many things that are important, may defeat our efforts for the spiritual welfare of our children. Prayer and personal obedience, instruction and correction of our children are all necessary and interrelated. Praying for our children without instructing them will not help them. If we instruct our children in godliness but are an example of ungodliness, our children will be confused. Our children will be able to discern and learn hypocrisy if we have prayed with our family but have never spent time in earnest private wrestling in our prayer closet. In fact, praying with and for our children, training them properly, and setting a good example, will all be negated if we allow them to be in places where they might be tempted and very likely destroyed.

---

[148] Philippians 1:23
[149] John 12:28

We must be prayerfully cautious about the attitudes we foster in our children concerning material possessions. Cotton Mather, a preacher in a large Boston church in colonial America, said, "Religion gives birth to prosperity and then the daughter devours the mother." John Wesley warned the Christians of his day, "Wherever riches have increased, the essence of religion has decreased in the same proportion. Therefore, I do not see how it is possible, in the nature of things, for any revival of religion to continue long. For religion must necessarily produce both industry and frugality, and these cannot but produce riches. But as riches increase so will pride, anger, and love of the world in all of its branches... Is there no way to prevent this—this continued decay of pure religion?"[150]

Love of material possessions in Christian families is one of the greatest hindrances to the spread of the Gospel. By their example, parents obsessed with acquiring possessions show their children that the things of this world are more important than the things of eternity. If parents give very little to the cause of Christ in proportion to what God has given them, their children will do the same. God has said: *"The silver is Mine, and the gold is Mine."*[151] Parents should teach their children that acquiring property has importance only if it is used to honor Christ. They should let their children see them giving regularly as God has prospered them.[152] Long after they are dead, their children will follow their example; therefore, they must leave them the legacy of their devoted spirit and Christ-honoring

---

[150] Quoted in Dean M. Kelley, *Why Conservative Churches are Growing*, Harper & Row Publishers, New York, 1972, p. 55.

[151] Haggai 2:8

[152] See 1 Corinthians 16:2.

habits. They must teach them that, *"It is more blessed to give than to receive."*[153] They must encourage them to write *"holiness to the Lord"*[154] upon their pocket books. Parents will be blessed as well, if they show their children, by example, that it is wise to practice simplicity and economy in dress, furniture, and style of living.

Wesley's question, "Is there no way to prevent this—this continued decay of pure religion?" is a hard one. The solution is simple in precept, but extremely difficult in practice. The decay of pure religion can be avoided by prayerfully determining what is necessary to properly care for one's household—spiritually and materially (i.e., food, clothing shelter, education, recreation, etc.)—and then to live accordingly. The numbers will vary from situation to situation. And what works for one family may not work for another. The important thing is that we prayerfully think it through and then live life accordingly. Then, as the Lord blesses with funds beyond what is needed for this standard, the additional resources are invested in ministry.

In this way, Christians consecrate their material possessions to Christ. When believers give Christ control of their material possessions, resources will be available to complete the Bride of Christ. As we give Christ total control of our money and possessions, we must not forget that we are also answerable to Christ for our children. Thousands of dollars are needed to carry on the work of evangelizing the world; but a thousand sanctified minds will do more than millions of dollars of money. When we teach our children to give of themselves, the Gospel will be

---

[153] Acts 20:35

[154] See Exodus 28:36; 39:30; Jeremiah 2:3 and Zechariah 14:20-21.

proclaimed in the *"dark places of the earth"* which *"are full of the haunts of cruelty."*[155]

We must avoid rigid legalism in our families. Some professing Christian parents have just enough religion to make them unhappy. Rigid legalism frustrates our efforts for the spiritual good of our children. Paul declared that though he was free from all men he made himself a servant to all, that he might win the more. Without compromising the truth, Paul became a Jew to the Jews that he might win Jews. To those who were under the law, Paul became as under the law, that he might win those who were under the law. To those who were without law, Paul became as without law that he might win those who were without law. To the weak, Paul became weak, that he might win the weak. Paul became all things to all men, that he might by all means save some.[156] Winning others to salvation requires Spirit-given winsomeness. Christian parents need a heavenly cheerfulness and sweetness, which shows our families that faith in Christ is a blessed and delightful reality.

Mothers have a special opportunity to bless children. Their duty and influence lies at the very heart of the work of training children for the service of Christ. A Christian mother may more richly bless the world through her children than many queens who have sat on thrones. To mothers, Divine Providence gives children for special care at the period of life when first and eternal impressions are made. Let your influence be *"sanctified by the word of*

---

155 Psalm 74:20

156 See 1 Corinthians 9:19-22.

God and prayer"[157] and consecrated to the high goal of equipping sons and daughters for *"the work of Christ."*[158]

There is no greater privilege than to train our children for the glory of Christ and the completing of His Bride. When this is our highest, most passionate desire, it gives focus to our instructions, corrections, and prayers. We will guard against every habit or influence that will hinder the accomplishment of this mission. We will teach our children godly self-denial, industry, and effort. We will not waver between Christ and the world. We will know why we train our children. Our children will know what they are living for; they will not be faithless to the goal set before them without violating their conscience. The Spirit of God often blesses such training with early conversion of our children, and thereby their whole lives are directed and used by God. Christian parents: *"Whatever your hand finds to do, do it with all your might."*[159]

There is no greater privilege than to train our children for the glory of Christ and the completing of His Bride. When this is our highest, most passionate desire, it gives focus to our instructions, corrections, and prayers.

• • • • •

---

[157] 1 Timothy 4:5

[158] See Philippians 2:29-30.

[159] Ecclesiastes 9:10 NIV

Stepping Over the Threshold

How do godly families survive in the midst of a hostile culture, in times of spiritual and social upheaval? Today it is apparent to any casual observer that the American culture is hostile to the home where Christ is Lord. Paul's promise to Timothy applies both to individuals and families. *"Yes, and all who desire to live godly in Christ Jesus will suffer persecution."*[160] The godly family has always been a threat to the forces of evil. So let us now turn to the task of learning more about how we can intercede for and with our family.

The Home as a Sanctuary

Perhaps we can learn how to respond to this onslaught by considering the Jewish people after the destruction of the temple in Jerusalem in 70 A.D. when the Jewish nation was scattered in exile. The rabbis saw the home as the key to survival. They began referring to the home as a "small sanctuary" or "miniature temple." It was at this time that Jewish fathers began seeing their home not as their castle, but as their sanctuary.

---

[160] 2 Timothy 3:12

As a small sanctuary, the rabbis taught that the home, like the temple, was to be set apart for special purposes. These included the worship of God (a house of prayer), the learning of the Torah or Law (a house of study), and serving the community needs (a house of assembly). Each home was to reflect God's glory through prayer, study, praise and mercy ministry.

After the destruction of the temple in Jerusalem in 70 A.D., the Jewish nation was scattered in exile. The rabbis saw the home as the key to survival. It was at this time that Jewish fathers began seeing their home not as their castle, but as their sanctuary. Each home was to reflect God's glory through prayer, study, praise and mercy ministry.

In the same manner that the earlier Israelites had come to the temple to celebrate festivals such as Passover, the Jews began to view the home as the center of religious life after the temple's destruction. The home was a place to celebrate holidays and festivals with joy and devotion. But it was more: the home provided an opportunity to inculcate religious values such as freedom and love for the Torah.

The Bible teaches that the family should be the main formative influence in the spiritual development of the individual. Not even the church can take the place of the home. The home bears primary responsibility for imparting Christian values and insuring godly nourishment and growth for each family member. In the words of

Moses, *"You* (fathers, not somebody else) *shall teach them* (God's commandments) *diligently to your children."*[161]

The Apostle Peter told the scattered Christians of his day, *"You are a chosen people (laos), a royal priesthood, a holy nation, a people belonging to God, that you may declare the praises of him who called you out of darkness into his wonderful light."*[162] All Christians are the *"laos"* or people of God. Christianity is a religion of lay people. It is not to be viewed or to function as merely a religion with paid professionals that are hired by congregations to perform religious duties and services.

This reality explains the survival of the Church in China. When the institutional churches were closed, missionaries exiled, and pastors murdered or imprisoned, the Church not only survived, it thrived. Today it numbers more than one hundred million believers. Christianity can always survive in the home if the family is diligent to worship God. The home, just like the Church, is made up of people—a community of priests ministering to God and to one another.

God explicitly commanded Moses that children be instructed in His word. This instruction was to be formal and casual, structured and spontaneous. Celebration of the Passover provided a time of structured family worship. Moses commanded, *"And it shall be, when your children say to you, 'What do you mean by this service?' that you shall say, 'It is the Passover sacrifice of the LORD, who passed over the houses of the children of Israel in Egypt*

---

[161] See Deuteronomy 6:7a.
[162] 1 Peter 2:9 NIV

when He struck the Egyptians and delivered our households.'" "So the people bowed their heads and worshiped. "[163]

Moses further instructed fathers to use daily living for casual, spontaneous instruction. *"And these words which I command you today shall be in your heart. You shall teach them diligently to your children, and shall talk of them when you sit in your house, when you walk by the way, when you lie down, and when you rise up. You shall bind them as a sign on your hand, and they shall be as frontlets between your eyes. You shall write them on the doorposts of your house and on your gates. "*[164]

When to Pray as a Family

When should you plan times of family worship—reading the Bible and praying for and with each other? Scripture tells us that morning and evening are the proper times for family worship.

David prayed in the morning. *"My voice You shall hear in the morning, O LORD; in the morning I will direct it to You, and I will look up. "*[165] The Psalmist also prayed every night. *"It is good to give thanks to the LORD, and to sing praises to Your name, O Most High; to declare Your loving kindness in the morning, and Your faithfulness every night, on an instrument of ten strings, on the lute, and on the*

---

[163] Exodus 12:26-27

[164] Deuteronomy 6:6-9   See also Deuteronomy 11:18-21.

[165] Psalm 5:3   See also Psalm 55:17; 88:13; 119:147; and Mark 1:35.

harp, with harmonious sound."[166]   *"Let my prayer be set before You as incense, the lifting up of my hands as the evening sacrifice."*[167]

Common sense tells us that morning and evening are the proper times for family worship. If you were to omit one, which would it be? Would you dare risk sending your families out into the world all the day without committing them to the care of Providence in the morning? Would you undertake your secular pursuits without pleading for divine blessing upon them? Each night when you pillow your head there is the possibility that you or members of your family will not awaken in this world but the next. How can you risk sleeping without committing yourselves and yours to the divine protection, and offering thanks for the mercies of the day?

Nature, as well, seems to direct us to these times. Life consists of so many days; a day is a kind of life and sleep at night is a kind of death. Shall we enter upon life in the morning without acknowledging the Author of our life? Or shall we, as it were, die in the evening and not commend our departing spirits into His hands? Night is a kind of pause, a stop in the progress of life, and it should cause us to reflect on death and move us towards our divine Preserver.

The prophet Amos hints that we should seek the Lord as the Author of the revolutions of night and day: *"He turns the shadow of death into morning and makes the day dark*

---

[166] Psalm 92:1-3
[167] Psalm 141:2

as night."[168]   That is, we should seek Him with the idea that He is the Provider of each day of our lives. So what time is as proper for this as morning and evening? I encourage you to strive to begin and conclude the day, as a family, with God.

Household heads that neglect family prayer are without excuse. Those who live without it, live as if they are without God in the world. Some professed believers object that family prayer takes too much time, and keeps families too long from their other business. George Whitfield, the noted preacher of the First Great Awakening, said such persons are of the same hypocritical spirit as the traitor Judas. Judas had indignation against Mary's devotion when she poured her ointment on the Lord Jesus. Judas asked, *"'Why was this fragrant oil not sold for three hundred denarii and given to the poor?' This he said, not that he cared for the poor, but because he was a thief, and had the money box; and he used to take what was put in it."*[169] In that day a denarius was a day's wage and three hundred denarii was a year's salary. Judas' pragmatic business sense contributed to his ultimate downfall. When we take such an attitude by neglecting prayer, we too are complaining from a poor spirit, robbing God, and contributing to our downfall.

God gives us 24 hours in every day. Should we not allow some small portion of it, morning and evening, to worship Him? It is God who gives men *"power to get wealth."*[170] The best way to prosper in this world is to secure His favor.

---

[168] Amos 5:8

[169] See John 12:3-8.

[170] See Deuteronomy 8:18.

And, our Lord Himself has promised that if we *"seek first the kingdom of God and His righteousness,"*[171] all outward gifts will be added unto us.

Is there any legitimate excuse for not doing this sacred duty? Does God not provide enough time for each of us to do His whole will? Will not God one day require us to give an account to Him for the stewardship of our families? On that day, will it suffice to say, "I did not have enough time to pray for and with my family?" The more pressing our temporal responsibilities, the more desperate is our need for divine help. No Christian head of a household can claim to be unqualified for such a work. Gifts and talents are developed by use, not by neglect.

God gives us 24 hours in every day. Should we not allow some small portion of it, morning and evening, to worship Him? Will not God one day require us to give an account to Him for the stewardship of our families? On that day, will it suffice to say, "I did not have enough time to pray for and with my family?"

How to Pray as a Family

All members of the household should receive benefit from participating in family worship. When little ones are involved, they should be able to understand what is

---

[171] Matthew 6:33

79

presented. Therefore, family worship should be conducted reverently, simply, and earnestly.

Jesus promised a particular blessing to joint prayer: *"Where two or three are gathered together in My name, I am there in the midst of them."*[172] And, *"Again I say to you that if two of you agree on earth concerning anything that they ask, it will be done for them by My Father in heaven."*[173] These promises and commands without a doubt include family prayer. Joshua clearly has his family in mind when he declares, *"As for me and my house, we will serve the LORD."*[174] Their resolve to *"serve the LORD"* included prayer with his family, which is one of the best ways they could serve Him.

In the time of Jesus and His apostles, devout families gathered around the table and sang songs in praise of the Holy One, as the choirs used to sing in Solomon's temple. The father served as the priest of his own sanctuary, instructing his family in the words of the Torah (the Law), as did the priests of old. He would instruct his family to share with God's people who were in need; i.e., to practice hospitality.[175] Add to this, the fact that we are commanded in the New Testament to *"pray continually,"*[176] and to *"be anxious for nothing, but in everything by prayer and supplication, with thanksgiving, let your requests be made*

---

[172] Matthew 18:20

[173] Matthew 18:19

[174] Joshua 24:15

[175] See Romans 12:13; 1 Peter 4:9; Leviticus 19:34; Isaiah 58:7; Job 31:32; Hebrews 13:2; James 2:14-17; and 1 John 3:17.

[176] 1 Thessalonians 5:17 NIV

known to God."[177]   Regular times of family worship are amplified by a worshipful attitude through all of a family's time together.   Parents can use the events of the day to exemplify how worship is to be carried forth into all that we do.

The head of the family should perform the priestly duty. Begin family worship with a brief prayer seeking God's presence and blessing.   Then read a short Bible passage. Next, the day's catechism, including Scripture, should be read aloud.   Reading is good preparation for prayer, and prayer is an excellent means to render reading more effectual.   The leader should draw out the thinking of each member of the household and then express his own thoughts.   If desired, two or three verses of a Psalm or a hymn may be sung.

Next, the leader should orchestrate prayer.   Every family has blessings for which to give thanks, afflictions they need to pray against, sins they need to confess.   It is difficult to imagine how family worship can be done without joining together in common acts of praise, humiliation, supplication, thanksgiving, and intercession.   Family members should not strive to pray eloquently or extensively; rather, they should pray with simplicity. Conversational prayer is usually best: one person prays a short sentence, then the next person picks up on the same subject and prays another sentence enlarging the subject. This continues until the subject is covered, then someone introduces another subject with another sentence-prayer. Conversational prayer makes it possible for all who so desire to enter into the conversation with God.   Beware of

---

[177] Philippians 4:6

wearying the young ones! The leader closes by placing the family into the hands of God.

Meaningful variety and special blessing can be added to family worship by observing holidays and special occasions, such as birthdays. There can be a special time of blessing with a celebration that includes gratitude to God for the birth of the family member. Birthdays thirteen and eighteen are special in a young person's life; becoming a teenager is a significant milestone, and legally becoming an adult brings with it new privileges and responsibilities. Holidays in the church calendar, such as Christmas, Easter, and Pentecost can provide a significant focus for family prayer. National holidays such as Memorial Day and Independence Day provide the opportunity to properly relate piety and patriotism.

Remember to keep daily family worship brief and to the point. On Sundays, however, more casual and extensive family time should be arranged. For instance, after attending morning worship services, the family might spend some relaxed time in the afternoon talking about the sermon, Christian issues, or other spiritual things. This is a perfect time for parents to work at developing a deeper spiritual relationship with their children.

Family Prayer— A Factor in Blessing and Cursing

Family worship helps prevent and resolve many sins. It provides a regular opportunity for children, and adults, to wipe the slate clean from transgressions against one another. In this atmosphere, children learn how to return a blessing for an insult.

Family worship encourages the soul, conveys a sense of God's majesty and authority, sets solemn truths before the mind, and brings benefits from God to the home. God uses personal faith in parents to build faith in children. To a great extent, this is because children are creatures of imitation; they love to copy what they see in others, especially when they are young.

> **Family worship helps prevent and resolve many sins. It provides a regular opportunity for children, and adults, to wipe the slate clean from transgressions against one another. In this atmosphere, children learn how to return a blessing for an insult.**

The Psalmist emphasizes this desire to keep our faith vital from generation to generation, *"For He established a testimony in Jacob, and appointed a law in Israel, which He commanded our fathers, that they should make them known to their children; that the generation to come might know them, the children who would be born, that they may arise and declare them to their children, that they may set their hope in God, and not forget the works of God, but keep His commandments."*[178]

Much of the moral and spiritual decay of the masses today may be traced back to fathers' neglecting this duty of family worship. Daily prayer in the home is a powerful means of grace for curbing the sinful appetites to which our fallen nature is attracted. It also provides a safety net of

---

[178] Psalm 78:5-7

prayer warriors, one for another, in battling the influences of the world, the flesh and the devil.

Family prayer gains for us the special presence and blessing of the Lord. Jesus promised, *"Again I say to you that if two of you agree on earth concerning anything that they ask, it will be done for them by My Father in heaven. For where two or three are gathered together in My name, I am there in the midst of them."*[179] Many have found in family worship the help and communion with God, which they sought and did not find in private prayer.

On the other hand, notice the terrible threats that are declared against all who disregard the duty of family prayer. Ponder Jeremiah's awe-inspiring words, *"Pour out Your fury on the Gentiles, who do not know You, and on the families who do not call on Your name."*[180] Sadly, many non-Christian families today are more consistent in the worship of their false gods than some professing Christians are in worshipping the True God. Think how regular and consumed some people are with things such as sports activities, sometimes even to the exclusion of public worship. Or look at how disciplined some may become in following after health fads, watching certain television programs, or collecting valuable possessions. To them, nothing is more important than what they have blindly chosen to put their faith in. Jeremiah asks God to pour out His fury—a chilling thought! And yet, to the extent that these descriptions may be accurate of some Christians, how loudly these words speak to us!

---

[179] Matthew 18:19-20
[180] Jeremiah 10:25

Preparing the Sanctuary

Have you become convinced to make daily family worship a priority? You should at this point have a practical game plan for how to implement this important aspect of your family's life. Let's look at some specific ways to make your home an outpost for ministry.

The Old Testament Hebrew word "*beth*" and Greek New Testament word "*oikos*" are variously translated into two English words: household (meaning family) and house (meaning the structure in which the family lives). This interchangeability indicates that people are closely related to the structure in which they live. The material house becomes a visible representation of the people who live in it. What does the house in which you live tell about you? The psalmist warned, *"Unless the LORD builds the house, they labor in vain who build it."*[181]

While we must not think of the home and the Church as buildings but as a community of people who regularly meet in the buildings, we must be aware of the influence buildings and material possessions have on our lives. Sir Winston Churchill said, "We shape our buildings; and afterwards our buildings shape us."[182] This principle also applies to all our material possessions. We acquire possessions, and if we do not periodically evaluate their impact on our lives, the possessions take more and more control of our lives. Most Americans now act as though things are more valuable than people, as judged by money

---

[181] Psalm 127:1

[182] Winston S. Churchill, 28 October 1943 to the House of Commons (meeting in the House of Lords).

and time spent. Having the latest model car is more important than raising children, and the size of one's bank account is more important than the health of one's marriage or family. Solomon, the wisest man who ever lived, warns, *"Many waters cannot quench love, neither can rivers drown it. If a man tried to buy love with everything he owned, his offer would be utterly despised."*[183]

While we must not think of the home and the Church as buildings but as a community of people who regularly meet in the buildings, we must be aware of the influence buildings and material possessions have on our lives.

Jesus warns, *"Watch out! Be on your guard against all kinds of greed; a man's life does not consist in the abundance of his possessions."*[184] Satan showed Jesus *"all the kingdoms of the world and their splendor."* *"All this I will give you,"* Satan said, *"if you will bow down and worship me.'"*[185] Paul reminds us that *"what is seen is temporary, but what is unseen is eternal."*[186] Satan still seeks to distract God's people from eternal realities with temporal trinkets.

A key to keeping an eternal perspective on our material possessions is to dedicate them to the Lord. That is why Scripture commands, *"Who is the man that has built a new*

---

[183] Song of Solomon 8:7 NLT

[184] Luke 12:15 NIV

[185] Matthew 4:8-9 NIV

[186] 2 Corinthians 4:18 NIV

house and has not dedicated it? Let him depart and return to his house, otherwise he might die in the battle and another man would dedicate it."[187]

Moses also commanded,

> *These words, which I am commanding you today, shall be on your heart. You shall teach them diligently to your sons and shall talk of them when you sit in your house and when you walk by the way and when you lie down and when you rise up. You shall bind them as a sign on your hand and they shall be as frontals on your forehead. You shall write them on the doorposts of your house and on your gates.*[188]

Devout Jewish people still keep this command. The Ten Commandments are written on a small parchment scroll and put in a prepared place in the doorframes of their home. This reminds them that their homes belong to God and that what happens in them is to be controlled by His word.

When Solomon dedicated the temple to the Lord, the Lord promised to respond to prayers offered there. *"My eyes will be open and My ears attentive to the prayer made in this place. For now I have chosen and sanctified this house, that My name may be there forever; and My eyes and My heart will be there perpetually.*"[189]

Therefore, it is reasonable to infer that God will answer prayer offered in dedicated homes. In homes, Paul and the

---

[187] Deuteronomy 20:5 NASB

[188] Deuteronomy 6:7-9 NASB

[189] 2 Chronicles 7:15-16

other Apostles preached the kingdom of God and taught concerning the Lord Jesus Christ: *"Every day, in the temple and from house to house, they* (the Apostles) *kept right on teaching and preaching Jesus as the Christ."*[190] Paul *"stayed two full years in his own rented quarters, and was welcoming all who came to him, preaching the kingdom of God and teaching concerning the Lord Jesus Christ with all openness, unhindered."*[191] In homes, many people gathered together to pray, preach, and teach the word of God: *"When he* (Peter) *realized this, he went to the house of Mary, the mother of John who was also called Mark, where many were gathered together and were praying."*[192]

Jewish people were taught about God from very early childhood to the grave. They realized they could never learn everything about the infinite God in one lifetime yet, they tried to know Him as well as possible. They knew they would be with Him for all eternity so they studied His word together every day in the temple and in their homes.

God and Your House

I encourage you to do as the Israelites did and dedicate your home to God and to His service. There is an exercise in *Appendix Two* on page 139, which will help you think through the implications of doing so.

God required specific preparation for the Day of Atonement. He commanded that each Jewish home be

---

[190] Acts 5:42 NASB

[191] Acts 28:30-31 NASB

[192] Acts 12:12 NASB

examined room by room to remove all yeast, which is a symbol of sin. *"For seven days you are to eat bread made without yeast. On the first day remove the yeast from your houses, for whoever eats anything with yeast in it from the first day through the seventh must be cut off from Israel. ...For seven days no yeast is to be found in your houses. And whoever eats anything with yeast in it must be cut off from the community of Israel, whether he is an alien or native-born. Eat nothing made with yeast. Wherever you live, you must eat unleavened bread."*[193] *"For seven days eat bread made without yeast and on the seventh day hold a festival to the* LORD. *Eat unleavened bread during those seven days; nothing with yeast in it is to be seen among you, nor shall any yeast be seen anywhere within your borders."*[194] *"Let no yeast be found in your possession in all your land for seven days."*[195]

It may be necessary to remove some items from your home, or to rearrange the display of things that formerly were given treasured, high-visibility spots. Perhaps God has convicted you and/or your family to do some spring-cleaning or sprucing up in order to make your home into the sanctuary that it is meant to be. Maybe you want to develop a family worship corner/center for your daily devotions, or create space for a neighborhood Bible study or some other type of hospitality event. Whatever it may be, treat this preparation as a solemn and joyous task. Be considerate of what the Lord may have laid on the heart of each member of the household—what might be a stumbling

---

[193] Exodus 12:15, 19-20 NIV

[194] Exodus 13:6-7 NIV

[195] Deuteronomy 16:4 NIV

block to some, may not be a stumbling block to all, but all stumbling blocks should be addressed.

It is a good idea for the family to go room-by-room, thinking about what items might represent *"yeast"* to you and your household; things which the Lord might desire you to get rid of. It is possible that others in the family will recognize something as *"yeast,"* to which you might be blind! A room-by-room review is provided in *Appendix Three*, on page 145, to assist you in this task. Do not tackle every room all at one time. It's better to take your time and do this process thoughtfully.

Following the survey are two exercises to help you reflect on your material possessions. The first will help you identify the three most important things in your home. The second is a study of Scripture designed to encourage you to weigh the future impact of your possessions on your heirs.

When you have finished preparations and everything is ready, a sample home dedication service is provided in *Appendix Four*.

God Will Use Your Home

When you and the members of your household dedicate your house to the Lord, expect Him to use it! Think about the things God did in homes in the Apostolic church. What does God desire to do in and through your home to bear witness to the watching world? Explore the list of possibilities below and prayerfully ask God which ones He wants you to do. Also, ask the Lord if there are other things not listed here which He might want you to do.

Home Dedication or Re-dedication

As you dedicate or rededicate your home, who do you think God would want you to witness to? Make a list of friends, neighbors, work associates, relatives, and begin praying for these people individually and during your family worship. Then invite them to your home dedication service.

When you and the members of your household dedicate your house to the Lord, expect Him to use it!

Evangelistic Entertainment

In the early church, Christians broke bread together often. Many unbelievers will attend a dinner, desert or party in a friend or neighbor's home when they would not go to a church to hear the gospel. Use occasions such as:

- a birthday party for a family member, friend, neighbor, or work associate
- an anniversary party to celebrate a marriage, or other significant milestone in someone's life
- a Congratulation Party upon the birth of a new child, advancement to a new position, etc.
- a holiday party celebrating Christmas, New Years, Memorial Day, Labor Day, etc.
- a neighborhood open house to rejoice over the completion of a remodeling project, to honor a person in the neighborhood such as a senior citizen, etc.
- a pizza and video party for Friday night fun or to share an interest between movie buffs
- fellowship meals to get to know another person or family better, to find things in common, etc.

At a minimum, these events will help to build relationships that are conducive for witnessing. They give opportunity for non-Christians to see the hope within Christians. When the party is held in honor of a committed believer, it might be possible to share a direct witness during the party. So, when you entertain, be sure to include non-Christians.

Bible Study Group

Throughout the history of the Church, Christians have found that meeting in homes to study the word of God is a great source of strength. Hosting a Bible Study can be a great help to your regular intake of the word, and it can teach your children the importance of this spiritual discipline.

Key Covenant Teams

These are small groups of Christians, who commit themselves to God and to one another, in order to study writings on revival. *The Spirit of Revival, Discovering the Wisdom of Jonathan Edwards,*[196] is a good text to start with. It is a modernized version of Edwards' *The Distinguishing Marks of a Work of the Spirit of God.* Edwards explains the five positive marks that are always present when the Holy Spirit is at work. These marks, drawn from 1 John 4, enable us to distinguish genuine revival from counterfeits.

---

[196] *The Spirit of Revival, Discovering the Wisdom of Jonathan Edwards*, Crossway Books, Wheaton, IL, 2000. The book contains a six-session discussion guide. A separate *Leader's Guide for The Spirit of Revival* is available from Serve International.

Prayer Groups

Praying and sharing with other Christians in a home prayer group could start a spark that might be fanned into a flame for great revival. *The Kingdom Campaign*[197] is a booklet describing how to develop the discipline of kingdom-focused prayer in a four-person fireteam. It also describes this book and other manuals in the Kingdom Campaign series, which can be used to guide your prayer time together. The principles and procedures set forth in the Kingdom Campaign can be used to transform your family and others into fruitful fireteams of kingdom intercessors.

Household Devotions

When a family reads the Bible and prays together on a regular basis, the entire living situation is affected. Include overnight guests in family worship when they are present!

Regular Household Council

People living under the same roof need to communicate with one another. A consistent, regularly scheduled time for dialog can be a great help to coordinate the family calendar, to resolve issues for family discussion, or to put together plans, ideas, hopes and dreams about the future. *Appendix Five* will aid in setting up the household council.

Garage Sale

A room-by-room review usually reveals that we have many things we no longer need. Selling the unused and

---

[197] Available from Serve International.

unnecessary things that collect in the house not only reduces clutter, but provides additional resources which can be used and are much needed for world evangelization.

Other Uses

The Holy Spirit may have brought to mind things not mentioned above, such as other opportunities to share your home in hospitality and mercy ministries. He can do some unique and exciting things if you ask Him to show you what He would like to accomplish through your home. Make a note of your ideas and share them with your family during a meeting of your household council.

A Visible Reminder

When God made a covenant with Noah, He put a rainbow in the sky as a visible reminder of His promise to bless Noah and all future generations. Later, when Moses passed God's law on to the Israelites, he told them to do similarly by writing God's words on the doorposts of their homes.

It is helpful to have a visible reminder of agreements we enter into with the Lord. A small plaque put in a prominent place in your home is a reminder to all members of the household that you have committed yourselves and your possessions to our loving, living Christ. The symbol is also a source of witness to non-believers entering your home.

Other ideas for reminders include using the Chinese character for "blessing," or the Hebrew word *Shalom*. Some use a small banner or plaque inscribed, "Holiness unto the Lord." Joshua 24:15, *"as for me and my house, we will serve the Lord,"* makes a wonderful reminder of your family's determination.

In this book, I hope that I have provided insight on how godly families in our present hostile American culture can survive and thrive. The key is for believers to pray with and for their families. Preparation, dedication and use of our homes will set the tone for family worship, witness and glory to God. Then whatever ministry God may guide us to establish in our homes, kingdom-focused prayer for and with our family will be the undergirding essential to withstanding our enemies—the world, the flesh and the devil.

I pray that these last ninety days have been a grace-driven, faith-growing delight. I hope they have been all you expected and more, helping to increase your joy and that of your household. May you continue on your daily journey in kingdom-focused prayer, and may you multiply after your kind—that is, develop others who will pray for and with their families.

Godly families can survive and thrive in our present hostile American culture. The key is for believers to pray with and for their families. Kingdom-focused prayer for and with our family will be the undergirding essential to withstanding our enemies—the world, the flesh and the devil.

•••••

Discussion Guide

Discussion Guide

Intercede For and With Your Family is the corporal's training manual for stage II of the Kingdom Campaign. To receive full benefit from this manual, you should have already completed the private's training manual in stage I (***Improve Your Prayer Life***) and you should now be using the training you received in stage I to help three people in your own fireteam transform their instinctive, reactive prayer into biblical, proactive kingdom-focused prayer. To properly lead your new fireteam, you must continue your 15 minutes (10 each morning and 5 each evening) of daily kingdom-focused prayer using what you learned from ***Improve Your Prayer Life***.[198] I would suggest that you add 5 more minutes to this private time each morning, praying for your family and for help in leading your fireteam. Spend the time asking the Lord to enable you lead your family in meaningful family worship. You can then spend 10 minutes at dinner, or whatever time is best for your household, praying with your family.

The following *Discussion Guide* has been prepared to help you plan how you will work through the material in this book, as well as how you will be enabled to achieve God's purpose for your family by investing an additional fifteen minutes daily in kingdom-focused prayer. Before you

---

[198] Archie Parrish, Serve International, Atlanta, GA, 2000.

begin reading the text, be sure to read the introductory material in this *Discussion Guide* (through the *Fireteam Commitment* on page 117), as it will answer many of the questions you may have, or will have! It also will explain how to use the *Daily Prayer Guide* (see *Appendix Six*), which should help you in using the Westminster Shorter Catechism for family worship.

Each session in the *Discussion Guide* provides instructions for materials to be completed prior to your monthly fireteam meeting.[199] For example, read and work through *Session One* before your team meets the first month. (Fireteams meet once a month, for three months; each meeting lasts two hours. It is assumed that you are familiar with the fireteam concept, and that you are studying this book using that format.)

Session instructions include, among other things, study questions to be read prior to reading the material in the text. They also include reading assignments, which will prepare you for discussion in your fireteam meetings. Approximately 35 pages of reading are assigned before each monthly meeting, or an average of 1 page per day. (To accomplish this task in five days each week, plan to read on the average of 1.5 pages each day.) Or perhaps you will want to take an hour once each week to accomplish this task. If you decide you want to cover the material in one sitting, do so early in the month so you can reflect on it during your prayer times throughout the month.

---

[199] For more information on fireteams, see *The Kingdom Campaign* booklet, available free from Serve International.

Six Learning Activities

Over the next ninety days, it will be best to continue the six activities you learned to use in *Improve Your Prayer Life*.[200] To refresh your memory, they are:

- Praying will make you a focused person.
- Reading will make you an informed person.
- Writing will make you an exact person.
- Meeting will make you a bonded person.
- Discussing will make you an insightful person.
- Doing will make you a growing person.

Praying Will Make You a Focused Person

Prayerful study focuses your mind on discovering God's will. At the beginning of each session, you will find the following printed prayer:

Lord, teach me, and my teammates, to pray with kingdom focus for and with our families. Give us helpful insights and understanding from what we study today. Show us what we need to understand better. As You show us things we are eager to try, enable us to do them. As You show us things that we find hard to apply to our lives, help us to be honest about them. Lord, as we review the questions in the *Discussion Guide*, focus our minds and help us find and obey the truth in what we study.

Start your study right now by meditating on this prayer; make its thoughts yours, and then pray it. Plural pronouns are used so that, in your thinking, you develop a kingdom

---

[200] Archie Parrish, Serve International, Atlanta, GA, 2000.

focus and include others. Write the names of your fireteam members, your family, your pastors and other church leaders, and a few church members and other Christians on the *Prayer List* provided in *Appendix One* on page 137. As you develop your *Prayer List,* don't make it so long that it becomes a burden.

When you study the assigned material, frequently pause and ask the Holy Spirit to give you understanding and discernment. Anytime you find your mind wandering, ask the Lord to refocus your thoughts. As He gives insight pause and ask Him for grace sufficient to do what He is telling you. Pray for your family and for opportunities to share what you learn with others. Pray that your fireteam members also would have opportunities to share with their potential recruits. Doing so will cause you to grow in what you are learning.

Reading Will Make You an Informed Person

The writer of the book of Hebrews states, "W*ithout faith it is impossible to please Him, for he who comes to God must believe that He is, and that He is a rewarder of those who diligently seek Him.*"[201]   What you receive from reading this book will, to a great degree, be determined by what you expect to receive. Read with expectant faith, and you will receive more of what God desires to give you. Before going any further, pause and complete this sentence in your mind: "From this book I expect to receive _____." Write your expectations on the *Prayer List* provided on page 137. When you finish reading the book, ask yourself if your expectations have been realized.

---

[201] Hebrews 11:6

As a member of a fireteam, you agree to read selected material according to a specific schedule. Start each session by rapidly reviewing the material in the *Discussion Guide* for that session. Then read the assigned portions of the book and write in your journal your answers to the *Four Filter Questions* found on page 104, as well as the answers to as many of the discussion questions as time permits.

Three Guards: Your mind will be fast at work as you read. But before you own anything in your heart, it must pass through three guards that protect your heart. Each guard is an automatic reaction; you may be unaware of it, yet you experience it. The three guards are as follows:

The Guard of Understanding: You must understand something to respond properly.

The Ethical Guard: After you understand something, it is more likely that you will do it if you believe it is right. You cannot do what you believe to be wrong without violating your conscience. God's word is *always* right, but some of its teachings may be hard for you to apply. When you find a hard saying, don't just pass over it. Make a note of it. Pray that God will help you properly respond. Share your concern with your fireteam and ask them to pray for you and help you.

The Emotional Guard: If you understand something and believe it is right, but fear that doing it will hurt you more than help you, you will struggle with doing it—or may not even try to do it. At times you will need to weigh apparent present benefits against actual eternal benefits. Paul put it this way: *"I consider that our present sufferings are not worth comparing with the glory that will be revealed in us."*[202]

Four Filter Questions: Four questions will help you think through and respond to your three guards. Tuck these in your mind:
1. What helpful insights do I understand from this section? (understanding)
2. What do I want to understand better? (understanding)
3. What is God telling me to do that I'm not afraid to try? (emotional)
4. What is God telling me that I find hard to apply to my life? (ethical or emotional)

You will be reminded to review these *Four Filter Questions* before you begin to read the text. The Bible tells us to search and we will find. Keeping these *Four Filter Questions* in mind will engage your mind to search for truth. At the end of your reading, react to your thoughts in light of these questions by writing your thinking in your journal.

As you read, it may be helpful to do the following:
1. Look for things that you understand and are eager to do. Place an asterisk (*) beside these.
2. Put a question mark (?) beside anything you do not understand.
3. Note anything that threatens you with an "X." Also indicate why it threatens you.

---

[202] Romans 8:18 NIV

Anytime you try to be what the Lord desires, the devil makes sure at some point you feel threatened. Deal with things that frighten you. *"For God has not given us a spirit of fear, but of power and of love and of a sound mind."*[203] If fear is there, face it with a sound mind (self-discipline), pray for spiritual empowerment, and it will vanish.

Writing Will Make You an Exact Person

Life that is worth living is worth recording. It is impossible to overestimate the increased benefit you will gain from each assignment if you will write down your responses to the *Four Filter Questions* and, as time permits, your responses to the questions from the *Discussion Guide*. Obviously, the more you put into this study, the more you will receive from it. When you are in a fireteam, sharing these written thoughts will bless you and others in the team.

All members of the fireteam keep a personal journal. Do not let the thought of writing your answers to the *Four Filter Questions* and the discussion questions in your journal overwhelm you. If you will try investing an average of 15 minutes a day in going through the text, you can easily work through all the material in a month's time.

Here are some practical suggestions for journal keeping:
- Do whatever works for you.
- Make journaling as convenient as possible.
- Carry a notebook for thoughts that occur to you during the day. Some prefer small notebooks they can carry in their coat pocket or purse. Others prefer to use a larger notebook.

---

[203] 2 Timothy 1:7

- If you write your journal in longhand, be sure to write enough to retain your full thought.
- If you are able to use a word processor and one is convenient for you, try it. But, if your access to it is limited, stick to old-fashioned handwriting.
- Don't worry about sentence structure, spelling, or penmanship. No one else will see your writing.
- Don't just copy words from the text. Express your thoughts in your own words.
- Throughout the *Discussion Guide*, you will see questions such as, "Do you agree? Why?" It is important to think these questions through. Don't blindly accept the thoughts in the text.

Now, before going any further, stop, take your journal, and copy from your *Prayer List* (on page 137) your answer to this statement: "From this book I expect to receive _____."

The *Fireteam Commitment* form on page 117 is for you to sign (if you have not already done so) as a reminder of your responsibilities to God and to the other members of your fireteam. Copy your *Fireteam Commitment* into your journal. Why? Before a man was crowned king over Israel, he was required to write the law of the covenant in his own hand. This reinforced his knowledge of his responsibilities under this covenant. This handwritten copy of the law was evidence that he willingly assumed the covenant's responsibilities.[204]

---

204 *"When he takes the throne of his kingdom, he is to write for himself on a scroll a copy of this law, taken from that of the priests, who are Levites. It is to be with him, and he is to read it all the days of his life so that he may learn to revere the LORD his God and follow carefully all the words of this law and these decrees."* Deuteronomy 17:18-19 NIV

Make journal-keeping a life-long habit, and you will find new depth in your relationship with Jesus.

Meeting Will Make You a Bonded Person

If you are not involved in a fireteam, consider joining one. Doing so will provide encouragement, understanding and accountability to you, as well as to others in the group. Remember that you will receive most from this effort if you regularly discuss this material with other believers. This may be challenging, but it should not be overwhelming.

Fireteams meet for three two-hour monthly meetings at an agreed upon time and place. The meeting place should be free from unnecessary distractions. It should be a place where you can easily talk to each other and pray.

Fireteam members pray for each other daily. If one is absent from the team meeting, the leader should make contact to see that the team member stays current on the matters of the fireteam. As members grow closer to one another, they ask to be encouraged for more and more significant matters in their lives. Becoming a kingdom intercessor is serious business! The devil will attack the members of the fireteam in a variety of ways—you need each other's support.

Discussing Will Make You an Insightful Person

In the fireteam meeting, the members discuss their written responses. The discussion should take about one hour of your two-hour meeting. You will probably not have time to discuss all the questions provided in the *Discussion Guide* for each session. Your fireteam leader will deal with specific questions, but most of the discussion time will be focused on responses to the *Four Filter Questions*. Be prepared to express your thinking in these small groups by reviewing your journal prior to the meeting, and, if necessary, consolidating your thoughts or choosing the three most significant issues you want to discuss. Important insights gained from the discussion should be noted in your journal.

Doing Will Make You a Growing Person

The Apostle James exhorts:

Do not merely listen to the word, and so deceive yourselves. Do what it says. Anyone who listens to the word but does not do what it says is like a man who looks at his face in a mirror and, after looking at himself, goes away and immediately forgets what he looks like. But the man who looks intently into the perfect law that gives freedom, and continues to do this, not forgetting what he has heard, but doing it—he will be blessed in what he does.[205]

It is an old saying that, "Knowledge is power." The words of James make it clear that knowledge without proper action is NOT power; rather it brings judgment! Maturity can always be determined by how long it takes us to do what we know is the will of God. The more mature Christian obeys more quickly, the less mature Christian takes longer.

Obedience is the supreme test of faith in God and reverence for Him. *"Samuel replied: 'Does the LORD delight in burnt offerings and sacrifices as much as in obeying the voice of*

---

[205] James 1:22-25

the LORD? *To obey is better than sacrifice, and to heed is better than the fat of rams.'*"[206] No one can sustain a right relationship with the Lord without obedience.   Every thought must be made captive to and obedient to Christ.[207] Nothing less than "wholehearted" obedience to the truth is acceptable to God.[208] Therefore, each team member seeks to do what he or she believes the Lord is directing. Specific action-steps should be shared with the group. Before the close of each meeting, time should be spent praying for one another. At the beginning of each session there should be a brief time of reporting on progress in these actions.

Insight will come to those who pray and read. Greater understanding will come to those who, in addition to prayer and reading, record their responses to the *Four Filter Questions* and the exercises in the *Discussion Guide* in a personal journal and then regularly meet to discuss this with other Christians. But, ultimate benefit will come only to those who add obedience to all these steps, and do God's will as He reveals it through this process.

The Discipline of Praying

In addition to studying the material in this book, it is important that you develop the ability to pray with a kingdom focus for and with your family. Plan to continue your discipline of daily prayer, scheduling an additional fifteen minutes each day. It would be best to add five

---

[206] 1 Samuel 15:22 NIV

[207] See 2 Corinthians 10:5.

[208] See Romans 6:17 NIV.

minutes in the morning interceding <u>for</u> your family and ten minutes at dinner interceding <u>with</u> your family. (This would be added to the ten minutes in the morning and five minutes in the evening, which were developed in ***Improve Your Prayer Life***.[209] The daily total would now be thirty minutes—15 in the morning and 15 in the evening). The *Suggested Daily Time Investment* chart on page 116 shows you how the first two stages of the Kingdom Campaign training help you build the discipline of 30 minutes of daily kingdom-focused prayer.

In your second 15 minutes, use the sample prayers below and the family devotions in the *Daily Prayer Guide* (in *Appendix Six*) to build on what you have used previously. Spend the five minutes you are adding each morning during this stage (II) as follows:
- Pray for the members of the fireteam you are leading.
- Pray for your family prayer time that will occur later that day.
- Pray for each member of your family.

As you undertake more-determined prayer, be wise, and expect the evil one to create challenges. Ask the Lord to help you do whatever is necessary to make this a delightful time for each member of the family. Here are various scriptural prayers for you to adapt and use in your own prayers:

<u>A prayer for the members of the fireteam you are leading</u>: (Think of them as members of your extended spiritual family.) Lord of the harvest, send

---

[209] Archie Parrish, *Improve Your Prayer Life,* Serve International, Atlanta, GA, 2000.

out workers into your harvest field.[210] Lord, pour out *"the Spirit of grace and supplication"* on my team members [211] Help them to pray daily and to seek faithful men and women *"who will be able to teach others also."*[212] Call three of those you have put on their hearts to be members of their fireteams in the next stage of the Kingdom Campaign in our church. Give them the desire and ability to teach others also.

A prayer for the whole family: Heavenly Father, from You Your whole family in heaven and on earth derives its name[213]. You urge us to *"come boldly to the throne of grace, that we may obtain mercy and find grace to help in time of need."*[214] You declare that Your *"grace is sufficient"* for us, for Your power is *"made perfect in weakness."*[215] Therefore, hear us as we call on You. We acknowledge that *"every good gift and every perfect gift"*[216] is from You. Help us make our home *"a house of prayer for all nations."*[217] May Your eyes be open and Your ears attentive to the prayer offered in this house. May Your name be honored here forever, and may Your eyes and Your heart be here perpetually.[218]

---

[210] Matthew 9:38 NIV; Luke 10:2 NIV

[211] Zechariah 12:10

[212] 2 Timothy 2:2

[213] Ephesians 3:14-15

[214] Hebrews 4:16

[215] 2 Corinthians 12:9

[216] James 1:17

[217] Mark 11:17

[218] 2 Chronicles 7:16

<u>A prayer for husbands and wives</u>: Help us pray daily for and with each other. You promised, *"Where two or three are gathered together in My name, I am there in the midst of them."*[219] And you said, *"that if two of you agree on earth concerning anything that they ask, it will be done for them by My Father in heaven."*[220] Be with us now. Like Joshua of old, we declare, *"As for me and my house, we will serve the LORD."*[221] Lord, enable us to live with each other, to love each other, to stay faithful to each other, to help each other, to be patient with each other, to encourage each other to trust Christ as Savior and Lord, to maintain intimacy, to look out for each other's interests in all things, to pray for each other, to seek and obey You Lord, and to keep ungodly materials out of our house.

<u>A husband's prayer</u>: Father, enable me to dwell with my wife according to understanding, giving honor to her as to the weaker vessel, and as being heirs together of the grace of life, that my prayers may not be hindered.[222]

<u>A wife's prayer</u>: Father, enable me today to respect my husband as a person, and for the position you have given him.[223] Help me to properly submit myself to him.[224]

---

[219] Matthew 18:20
[220] Matthew 18:19
[221] Joshua 24:15
[222] 1 Peter 3:7
[223] Ephesians 5:33
[224] Ephesians 5:22

<u>A parent's prayer</u>: Father, enable us to arise, cry out in the night, at the beginning of the watches; pour out our hearts like water before Your face, Lord. Help us to lift our hands toward You for the life of our children.[225] You promised, *"I will pour My Spirit on your descendants, and My blessing on your offspring; they will spring up among the grass like willows by the watercourses. One will say, 'I am the LORD'S'; another will call himself by the name of Jacob; another will write with his hand, 'The LORD'S,' and name himself by the name of Israel."*[226] Enable us as a family to call on Your name so that You will not pour out Your fury on us.[227] Father, enable our child/children/grandchildren to consciously depend on Your grace to overcome sin's impact in their lives. By Your Holy Spirit conform them to the likeness of Christ. Use them today in Your service with a single focus on Your glory.

<u>A father's prayer</u>: Father, turn my heart to my children, and turn the hearts of my children to me, lest You come and strike the earth with a curse.[228] You commanded me to teach Your word to my children, that my grandchildren might know it, and declare it to their children, that all my descendents might set their hope in You, and not forget Your works, but keep Your commandments.[229] Help me to do this.

---

[225] Lamentations 2:19
[226] Isaiah 44:3-5
[227] Jeremiah 10:25
[228] Malachi 4:5-6
[229] Psalm 78:5-7

For your family worship and prayer together, at dinner in the evening (or whenever is best for your family), spend ten minutes using this format:

- Opening sentence prayer.
- Read aloud from Scripture—Psalm 119, for instance.
- Read aloud the daily catechism (including Scripture) from the *Daily Prayer Guide* (in *Appendix Six*).
- Discuss the implications of these truths.
- Thank God for His truth, confess shortcomings, and ask for His help.
- Orchestrate conversational prayer for family members' needs.
- Close in a sentence prayer, placing the family into the hands of God.

The material in the *Daily Prayer Guide* (in *Appendix Six)* will take ninety days to complete. Don't be discouraged if you miss a day in this schedule; continue to ask the Lord to enable you. If you miss a day during the week, you might be able to have more extended time on Sunday.

The head of the household leads. Keep daily family worship brief and to-the-point. Draw out the thinking of each member of the household and encourage the expression of those thoughts. Family members take turns reading the passage from Psalms, the catechism questions, answers and Scriptures. Guard against talking about prayer but not praying. Discuss implications of specific truth, thank God for it, confess where they fall short and ask His help. Don't ask for prayer requests but ask each person to express need in conversational prayer and for family members to support each other in these requests. As time permits, the leader may share relevant thoughts from his journal entries on *Improve Your Prayer Life* and *Intercede For and With Your Family.*

Think of your daily prayer time and your family worship as appointments with Jesus ... and keep them! This is especially important when you are trying to bring the family together. It seems that the larger number of people there are in the family, the more difficult it is to get them all present. Don't leave family worship for spare minutes, but plan a set time, continually making the effort to establish this discipline.

Again, I encourage you—and challenge you—to make the next ninety (90) days a period of extraordinary kingdom-focused prayer for and with your family. Ask God to make your home *"a house of prayer for all nations"*[230]—an outpost of heaven in a hostile fallen world! By the end of three months, daily kingdom-focused prayer for and with your family will be an automatic part of your life.

•••••

---

[230] Mark 11:17

Suggested Daily Time Investment
(in minutes)

	Stage	
	I	II
Early Morning	10	10+5
Dinner		+10
Evening	5	5
Total	15	30

Stage I: You begin to improve your prayer life using *A Simple Way to Pray*[231] to develop the discipline of praying 15 minutes a day, 10 in the morning and 5 in the evening.

Stage II: You intercede for and with your family, adding 15 minutes of daily prayer time, 5 in the morning interceding <u>for</u> your family and 10 at dinner interceding <u>with</u> your family using the *Daily Prayer Guide*.[232]

---

[231] Found in *Improve Your Prayer Life,* Archie Parrish, Serve International, Atlanta, GA, 2000.
[232] See *Appendix* Six—from the *Westminster Shorter Catechism.*

Fireteam Commitment

I desire to become a person of prayer—biblical, proactive, kingdom-focused prayer for and with my family. To this end, I covenant with the Lord and members of my fireteam to meet _____ times:

_____

_____

_____.

(insert scheduled dates and times)

With God's help, I will continue to pray 15 minutes daily, interceding for those on my *Prayer List* (see page 137). I will pray that my team members and I will become persons of prayer. I will read the selected material as scheduled. I will write my responses to the *Four Filter Questions* and as many of the discussion questions as time allows. I will meet with the other members of my team at

_____

(insert scheduled location)

to discuss this material and to learn to pray with a kingdom focus for and with my family 15 minutes daily. I will also continue the 15-minute discipline of praying I learned in *Improve Your Prayer Life*, thus spending a total of 30 minutes daily in kingdom-focused prayer.

_____

Signature   Date

Session One

Before you begin to prepare for this session, pray:

Lord, teach me, and my teammates, to pray with kingdom focus for and with our families. Give us helpful insights and understanding from what we study today. Show us what we need to understand better. As You show us things we are eager to try, enable us to do them. As You show us things that we find hard to apply to our lives, help us to be honest about them. Lord, as we review the questions in the *Discussion Guide*, focus our minds and help us find and obey the truth in what we study.

I. If you have not read the booklet, **The Kingdom Campaign**,[233] please do so before your next fireteam meeting. This booklet explains why this ministry is necessary and how to implement it.

II. Read *Before You Begin* starting on page 11 and the introductory remarks of this *Discussion Guide* (pages 99 through 117). As necessary, review the *Six Learning Activities* found on page 101, and use them as you prepare for *Session One* with your fireteam. Review the questions below for each section <u>before</u> you

---

[233] Available free from Serve International.

read it. This will put your mind in search mode and enable you to get more from your reading.

III. Write the following Scriptures on a card. Carry it with you and read it aloud frequently. You will be asked to recite or read these verses in your fireteam meeting.

The Lord God said, 'It is not good that man should be alone; I will make him a helper comparable to him.' ...Therefore a man shall leave his father and mother and be joined to his wife, and they shall become one flesh. (Genesis 2:18, 24)

The Lord has been witness between you and the wife of your youth, with whom you have dealt treacherously; yet she is your companion and your wife by covenant. But did He not make them one, having a remnant of the Spirit? And why one? He seeks godly offspring. Therefore take heed to your spirit, and let none deal treacherously with the wife of his youth. For the Lord God of Israel says that He hates divorce, for it covers one's garment with violence, says the Lord of hosts. "Therefore take heed to your spirit, that you do not deal treacherously." (Malachi 2:14-16)

IV. Review the *Four Filter Questions* found on page 104. Read *The Family's Present Plight* and *God's Design for the Family* (pages 15 through 36) and write in your journal the answers to the *Four Filter Questions*.

V. Answer as many of the following questions as time allows.

The Family's Present Plight

1. Charles Colson observes that our responses to the "systematic deconstruction" of the family are more "reactive rather than proactive." (See page 15.) Does that generalization address you and your responses to our culture's assault on your family? List some ways you have "reacted." List some ways you can respond more "proactively."

2. What do most long-term prison inmates have in common? (See page 16.) Why do you think this is true?

3. Pretend that a good friend of yours announces to you that he or she is pursuing a divorce and that everyone involved will be better off. Using Scripture and the statistics Charles Colson identifies, write a letter to your friend, dispelling that premise.

4. "Our practice of prayer during our engagement continued into a daily practice in marriage." (See page 23.) If you are married, do you pray with your spouse daily? Why or why not? Perhaps this is a question that you might want to discuss with your spouse.

God's Design for the Family

5. A family is "the core institution of human society—the training ground, in fact, for all other social institutions." (See page 26.) In what ways is your family life a training ground for all other social institutions? Write out a narrative of a recent example of this kind of training that took place in your family.

6. "God uses His spiritual family, the Church, to strengthen physical families, and He uses physical families to reinforce His spiritual family, the Church." (See page 29.) Explain why you agree or disagree with this statement.

7. "Family prayer and worship is the God-preferred means for developing godly offspring." (See page 29.) Explain why you agree or disagree with this statement.

8. Describe your understanding of the parent's role in the evangelization of their children. (See page 32.)

9. "We cannot think we have faithfully discharged our responsibility while we neglect to maintain our faith in front of our families." (See page 32.) Is there a specific habit or behavior in your life that could be a stumbling block to the children watching you?

10. Write a brief description of godly role models you had or have.

11. What is your understanding of the statement that "In providing for one's family, there must be a balance of provision for both material and spiritual necessities"? (See page 35.) Do you believe your family would all agree that there is balance between these two in your home?

12. Even if a person did not have godly role models in their own families when he or she was growing up, there are many biblical marriage and parenting skills which can be learned (e.g., regular daily worship, emotional maturity, budgeting, diet, time management, social/recreational balance, communication, etc.).

What are you doing to improve your training in these areas? (Singles, you can be working on these things also.)

13. Scripture states that parents are obligated to provide for the needs of their families. (See page 34) "Some use this command to provide for their families to justify their obsessive pursuit of material things." The key word in this sentence is "obsessive." Are their "obsessive pursuits of material things" in your life? Write down one that you believe God might want you to get His perspective on, and how you believe He might want you to do so.

•••••

Session Two

Before you begin to prepare for this session, pray:

> Lord, teach me, and my teammates, to pray with kingdom focus for and with our families. Give us helpful insights and understanding from what we study today. Show us what we need to understand better. As You show us things we are eager to try, enable us to do them. As You show us things that we find hard to apply to our lives, help us to be honest about them. Lord, as we review the questions in the *Discussion Guide*, focus our minds and help us find and obey the truth in what we study.

I. Review the *Six Learning Activities* found on page 101 and use them as you prepare for *Session Two* with your fireteam. Review the questions below for each section <u>before</u> you read it. This will put your mind in search mode and enable you to get more from your reading.

II. Write the following Scriptures on a card. Carry it with you and read it aloud frequently. You will be asked to recite or read this verse in your fireteam meeting.

Nevertheless let each one of you in particular so love his own wife as himself, and let the wife see that she respects her husband. (Ephesians 5:33)

125

If it seems evil to you to serve the Lord, choose for yourselves this day whom you will serve, whether the gods which your fathers served that were on the other side of the River, or the gods of the Amorites, in whose land you dwell. But as for me and my house, we will serve the Lord. (Joshua 24:15)

III. Review the *Four Filter Questions* found on page 104. Read *Our God-given Responsibilities* (pages 37 through 72) and write in your journal the answers to the *Four Filter Questions*.

IV. Answer as many of the following questions as time allows. Don't pass on a particular question if your first impression is that it does not relate to you. You might be surprised what insights you may have for others in that situation.

Our God-Given Responsibilities

1. How and why should a husband love his wife biblically? (See page 38.)

2. List three practical examples of how a husband might lead "in loving humility." (See page 39.) How might leading in this way encourage wives to grow in willing submission?

3. List three practical examples of how a wife might demonstrate "respect" for her husband. How are "husbands more likely to change for the good if their wives respect them properly," i.e., biblically? (See page 39.)

4. "Marital love ... must be based on God's commands because they never change." (See page 42). If you are married, write this down in your own handwriting. Place it where you will see it regularly, and try rereading it to yourself when you see it. Satan, this world and your flesh will constantly be telling you of all the things they believe you should base your love for your spouse on. We all need a regular reminder of the truth.

5. "We owe patience to all, but especially to our spouse." (See page 46.) Many people are infinitely more patient with everyone else in their lives than they are with those in their own household. How patient are you with your family? Do you get angry often? Do you handle your anger in a biblical manner? If not, discuss this with your family and pray about it together. Seek assistance and guidance from your pastor, if necessary, to deal with reoccurring impatience and uncontrolled anger in your home.

6. The advent of the Internet has been the downfall of many people, especially men, in the area of maintaining sexual integrity. Pornography is now easily accessed in the privacy of the home or office and the temptation has been too great for many. Many church leaders have fallen prey. Is this a problem area for you? If so, take action at once to remove this temptation from your life. You can acquire low-cost software filters. Ask someone to hold you accountable, to encourage and support you to create firewalls from this temptation, and to pray for you.

7. "Husbands and wives must seek times for prayer together." (See page 51.) Note that the author says

couples must "seek" time to pray together. With schedules as busy as they are, those times will not create themselves. Talk with your spouse to decide the time of the day that will be best for the two of you to come together each day to pray. Write this time on your appointment calendars, and start to make that appointment a priority. If you are not married, find yourself a prayer partner of the same gender, and do the same.

8. The world teaches that marriage is a 50/50 relationship. Although that may sound "fair," it is not biblical. "Both parties must give 100%, regardless of whether or not the other spouse is 'giving.'" (See page 52.) Describe how a 50/50 relationship is different from one where both parties give 100%.

9. "Christians should abstain from anything that strikes either at faith or holiness—their own or their family's." (See page 53.) How well do think Christians today are doing at managing temptation in their homes? In their communities? In their world? How well are you and your family doing in this area?

10. Describe how Job provided a godly example in his home. (See page 56.)

11. How did Abraham exhibit a model of family worship? (See page 56.)

12. Joshua records a motto for leading his family in holiness. What was his commitment? (See page 58.)

13. "The first responsibility of parents is to instruct their children. ... We can never relinquish our own

responsibility to teach them biblical truth, and to monitor the teaching they receive from all other sources." (See page 63.) Many parents seem to believe that taking their children to Sunday School fulfills this responsibility. Do you agree or disagree with this position? Why?

14. "All our work as parents should begin at the throne of grace." (See page 64.) Do you think that most Christian parents pray regularly for their children, and for their own wisdom, strength, and commitment to this weighty task? If not, why do you think they don't?

15. "Parents obsessed with acquiring possessions show their children that the things of this world are more important than the things of eternity." (See page 69.) How large a problem do you believe this to be in the Christian community today? Is this a factor in your home? If so, what are some specific actions you might pray about taking to correct this miscommunication to your children?

16. "We must avoid rigid legalism in our families. Rigid legalism frustrates our efforts for the spiritual good for our children." (See page 71.) Which, if any, of the questions above raises a "red flag" in this area of legalism? What is the danger in legalism?

•••••

Session Three

Before you begin to prepare for this session, pray:

> Lord, teach me, and my teammates, to pray with kingdom focus for and with our families. Give us helpful insights and understanding from what we study today. Show us what we need to understand better. As You show us things we are eager to try, enable us to do them. As You show us things that we find hard to apply to our lives, help us to be honest about them. Lord, as we review the questions in the *Discussion Guide*, focus our minds and help us find and obey the truth in what we study.

I. Review the *Six Learning Activities* found on page 101 and use them as you prepare for *Session Three* with your fireteam. Review the questions below for each section before you read it. This will put your mind in search mode and enable you to get more from your reading.

II. Write the following Scriptures on a card. Carry it with you and read it aloud frequently. You will be asked to recite or read this verse in your fireteam meeting.

> *You are a chosen people, a royal priesthood, a holy nation, a people belonging to God, that you may*

131

declare the praises of him who called you out of darkness into his wonderful light. (1 Peter 2:9)

Unless the Lord builds the house, they labor in vain who build it. (Psalm 127:1)

III. Review the *Four Filter Questions* found on page 104. Read *Stepping Over the Threshold* (pages 73 through 96) and write in your journal the answers to the *Four Filter Questions.*

IV. Answer as many of the following questions as time allows.

Stepping Over the Threshold

1. "Today it is apparent to any casual observer that the American culture is hostile to the home where Christ is Lord." (See page 73.) List two examples you have personally observed of how today's culture is hostile to the home where Christ is Lord.

2. Praying for and with your family implies a three-fold goal: 1) praying <u>for</u> your family (alone with God); 2) praying <u>with</u> your spouse (if you are married); and 3) praying <u>with</u> your family (if you have children in your home). In order to realize this goal, you must plan when each of these parts will be accomplished. Write down the days and times of the day that you plan for the next 30 days to do each. After that 30 days, re-evaluate for the next 30-day period, and so on until this goal becomes a routine in your household. NOTE: Missing a day is not necessarily a disaster. Repeatedly canceling due to a scheduling conflict will destroy the

development of the routine and likely manifest itself in guilt and frustration. Set the appointments and strive to be faithful to keep them.

3. With today's busy schedules, praying with your family (family worship) will probably be the most difficult part of your goal. What kind of adjustments might need to be made to accommodate this important activity? If you need to begin with a weekly time together on Sunday afternoon, for instance, how could you turn that into two or three gatherings each week? Write down your plans for family worship, and schedule your goal for a starting date, if you are not doing so now. Write this date on your *Prayer List* (see page 137) and begin to pray for it, knowing that the world, the flesh, and the devil will not support you in achieving this goal.

4. List six benefits of family worship and prayer. (See pages 82 through 84.)

5. "We acquire possessions, and if we do not periodically evaluate their impact on our lives, the possessions take more and more control of our lives." (See page 85.) List ways you and your family may struggle with the "priority of possessions" in your home.

6. If you have not already done so, complete *Appendix Two*. Have you been convinced to dedicate your home to God and to His service? If not, explain why not.

7. A room-by-room review (in *Appendix Three*) is strongly recommended. Describe your findings.

8. Schedule the launch of your dedication process (see *Appendix Four*) on your family calendar. Write down

that date, and begin, as a family, to pray for this process during your family worship time.

9. Were you encouraged to plan an evangelism event in your home? (See page 91.) If not, why not? If so, schedule a date for this event, begin to plan for it as a family, and be sure to include prayer for this event during your family worship. Make it a "family" event.

10. Several uses for your home were listed on pages 91 through 94. Are you currently using your home for any of these evangelistic or discipling purposes? If not, what might you begin to do? Make it a part of your family worship to "brainstorm" and pray about ideas for your family and home. *"As for me and my house, we will serve the LORD."*[234]

•••••

_____

[234] Joshua 24:15

Appendices

Appendix One

My Prayer List

From this book, I expect to receive

_____

_____

_____

Fireteam Members

1._____

2._____

3._____

Family Members

1._____

2._____

3._____

4._____

Pastors

1._____

2._____

Church Leaders

1._____

2._____

3._____

4._____

5._____

6._____

Church Members and Other Christians

1._____

2._____

3._____

4._____

5._____

6._____

Appendix Two

Two Questions to Consider in Dedicating Your Home to God and His Service

Have you dedicated to the Lord the house in which you
 live?

Yes   Because people forget, covenants need to be
        renewed periodically. People receive from
        covenants what they invest in them.
        Periodic renewal of covenants provides
        opportunity to evaluate how well you are
        doing. As a part of your covenant with the
        Lord, consider rededicating your home
        annually. Ask God to guide you to new
        ministry in and through your home. As a
        part of your home rededication, consider
        doing a *Room-by-Room Review* found in
        Appendix Three.

No   Dedicating the house is the responsibility of
        the head of the household. If you are the
        head of your household try to make
        dedicating your house a family affair.
        People who are single or who live alone are
        the head of their household.

        If you are a husband whose wife is not a
        believer, discuss dedicating your house with
        her. Do not demand that she dedicate the

house. An unbeliever may have great misunderstanding as to what dedicating your house will involve. Go through the *Room-by-Room Review* beginning on page 145 with her. If she is agreeable, proceed. If not, follow the instructions of Ephesians 5:25-33 and 1 Peter 3:7.[235] Claim the promise of Acts 16:31 for your household and pray toward the day when you can together dedicate your house.

If you are believing parents and your children are not believers, gather the family and discuss dedicating your house. Try to help them understand and to want to do this. If dedicating your house will mean a great change in life-style, expect some resistance. However, lovingly and prayerfully proceed.

---

[235] *"Husbands, love your wives, just as Christ loved the church and gave himself up for her to make her holy, cleansing her by the washing with water through the word, and to present her to himself as a radiant church, without stain or wrinkle or any other blemish, but holy and blameless. In this same way, husbands ought to love their wives as their own bodies. He who loves his wife loves himself. After all, no one ever hated his own body, but he feeds and cares for it, just as Christ does the church—for we are members of his body. 'For this reason a man will leave his father and mother and be united to his wife, and the two will become one flesh.' This is a profound mystery—but I am talking about Christ and the church. However, each one of you also must love his wife as he loves himself, and the wife must respect her husband.* (Ephesians 5:25-33 NIV) *Husbands, in the same way be considerate as you live with your wives, and treat them with respect as the weaker partner and as heirs with you of the gracious gift of life, so that nothing will hinder your prayers.* (1 Peter 3:7 NIV)

If you are a believing wife and your husband is not a believer or is unwilling to dedicate your house, do not force the issue. You cannot dedicate your house without his leadership. Follow the instructions of 1 Peter 3:1-6 and Ephesians 5:22-24.[236] Claim the promise of Acts 16:31 for your household and pray continuously for him. When he believes and/or is willing, then together you can dedicate your house.

If you are an adult member of the household but not the head, discuss the possibility of dedicating the house with the household head. If he or she is willing, proceed. If not, begin praying for God to move in the circumstances and give the desire to dedicate the house to the head person.

---

[236] *"Wives, in the same way be submissive to your husbands so that, if any of them do not believe the word, they may be won over without words by the behavior of their wives, when they see the purity and reverence of your lives. Your beauty should not come from outward adornment, such as braided hair and the wearing of gold jewelry and fine clothes. Instead it should be that of your inner self, the unfading beauty of a gentle and quiet spirit, which is of great worth in God's sight. For this is the way the holy women of the past who put their hope in God used to make themselves beautiful. They were submissive to their own husbands, like Sarah, who obeyed Abraham and called him her master. You are her daughters if you do what is right and do not give way to fear.* (1 Peter 3:1-6 NIV) *Wives, submit to your husbands as to the Lord. For the husband is the head of the wife as Christ is the head of the church, his body, of which he is the Savior. Now as the church submits to Christ, so also wives should submit to their husbands in everything* (Ephesians 5:22-24 NIV)

Would you like to dedicate or rededicate the house in which you live to the Lord?

No   I do not desire to dedicate the house in which I live to the Lord. If you can, but do not desire to, think about this: Should a person who will not give his earthly home to God for their few short years on earth expect God to give him a heavenly home for all eternity?

Yes   but I cannot. Find another believer who will join you in asking God to work in the lives of others who do not desire to dedicate your home (therefore making a house dedication impossible).

Yes   and my family agrees with me. Read through the material below, then gather the members of your household together and begin.

    Give each member of the household a copy of this guide to work through individually.
Ask each member of the household to spend seven days considering the possessions in your house and their effect on your household.

    If there are small children in your household, talk with them about the parts that are meaningful to them, and write down their thoughts for them.

At the end of the seven days, call the household council together. Discuss the results of your individual evaluations.

(A word of caution: Anytime you try to be what God wants, Satan will try to stop you. James gives good advice for anyone working through the matter of house dedication: *"God opposes the proud, but gives grace to the humble. Submit yourselves, then, to God. Resist the devil, and he will flee from you. Come near to God and he will come near to you."*[237]

•••••

---

[237] James 4:6-8 NIV

Appendix Three

Room-by-Room Review

Answer by circling the most appropriate number. An asterisk (*) is used throughout the review to remind you to write your thoughts in a notebook so you can share them in your household council. All family members (who are able) should do this exercise, considering their own and each other's perspectives.

Living Room/Family Room/Den

These rooms symbolize the need for loving relationships and vital communication between people who live in the same house and friends and neighbors who live elsewhere.

1. The members of our household relate well to each other.
   Strongly disagree   Strongly agree
       1   2   3   4   5

   *Why did you give this rating? What can be done to improve it?

2. The members of our household relate well to friends and neighbors.
   Strongly disagree   Strongly agree
       1   2   3   4   5

   *Why did you give this rating? What can be done to improve it?

Dining Room/Kitchen/Food

After the destruction of the temple in 70 A.D., the dinner table of Jewish homes became the altar of the home temple. Eating was to be more than a physical function; it was to be a spiritual instrument of religious service. Seen as an altar, the table was to be a place where more than food was to be passed; it was to be consecrated and set apart, a place where the words of the Torah (the Law) might be exchanged because *"man shall not live by bread alone."*[238]

3. The quantity of our family meals is proper.
   Strongly disagree   Strongly agree
      1   2   3   4   5

4. The quality of our family meals is excellent.
   Strongly disagree   Strongly agree
      1   2   3   4   5

5. The cost of our family meals is reasonable.
   Strongly disagree   Strongly agree
      1   2   3   4   5

6. Our family shares the work of meals (cooking, washing dishes, etc.).
   Strongly disagree   Strongly agree
      1   2   3   4   5

   *Why did you give these ratings? What can be done to improve them?

---

[238] Deuteronomy 8:3; cf. Matthew 4:4, Luke 4:4

7. There is no waste of our family meals.
   Strongly disagree   Strongly agree
       1   2   3   4   5

   *Why did you give this rating? What can be done to improve it?

8. We express meaningful appreciation to God at each meal.
   Strongly disagree   Strongly agree
       1   2   3   4   5

   *Why did you give this rating? What can be done to improve it?

9. We always express gratitude to the one who prepared the meal.
   Strongly disagree   Strongly agree
       1   2   3   4   5

   *Why did you give this rating? What can be done to improve it?

Grace at meals should be a normal part of a Christian's daily life. Some say grace at meals because they developed the habit in childhood. Others say grace before meals served at home, but not in public places. Have you ever thought through why Christians give thanks before eating? What is the biblical basis for doing so?[239]

10. We have meaningful conversation during meals.
   Strongly disagree   Strongly agree
        1   2   3   4   5

11. We invite unbelievers to dine with us often.
   Strongly disagree   Strongly agree
        1   2   3   4   5

12. We invite believers to dine with us often.
   Strongly disagree   Strongly agree
        1   2   3   4   5

*Why did you give these ratings? What can be done to improve them?

---

[239] Christianity is rooted in Jewish beginnings. For both Jews and Christians, prayer is the means by which God's people stay attuned to the truth that all of life is sacred. The *Talmud*, containing ancient Jewish traditions, tells us that a blessing for food was first articulated by Moses in gratitude for the manna that the Israelites ate in the desert (See Exodus 16.). Ancient rabbis taught, "It is forbidden to a man to enjoy anything of this world without a benediction, and if anyone enjoys anything of this world without a benediction, he commits sacrilege." Doing so would be the same thing as taking something that doesn't belong to us without the permission of the owner. This is so because no aspect of life is devoid of God's presence. *"The earth is the LORD'S, and everything in it, the world, and all who live in it."* (Psalm 24:1 NIV)

An increasing number of Christians around the world are fasting one day each week. This helps one empathize with those who are hungry. Also, the money saved can be sent to agencies that are helping to feed the starving.

13. I would you like to fast one day a week for a specified period of time.
    Strongly disagree   Strongly agree
         1   2   3   4   5

14. Our household devotions are excellent.
    Strongly disagree   Strongly agree
         1   2   3   4   5

   *Why did you give these ratings? What can be done to improve them?

Bedrooms

15. Our family observes proper sleeping times.
    Strongly disagree   Strongly agree
         1   2   3   4   5

16. Our bedrooms are free of clutter.
    Strongly disagree   Strongly agree
         1   2   3   4   5

17. The furnishings in our bedrooms are modest.
    Strongly disagree   Strongly agree
         1   2   3   4   5

   *Why did you give these ratings? What can be done to improve them?

18. All members of our family have excellent personal daily devotions.
    Strongly disagree   Strongly agree
       1   2   3   4   5

    *Why did you give this rating? What can be done to improve it?

Bathrooms

19. Our family members are considerate of others (not taking unnecessary time, not leaving clutter, etc.).
    Strongly disagree   Strongly agree
       1   2   3   4   5

20. Our family uses cosmetics of modest expense.
    Strongly disagree   Strongly agree
       1   2   3   4   5

21. Our family members do not try to substitute tranquilizers and pep pills for the fruit of the Spirit (peace and joy).
    Strongly disagree   Strongly agree
       1   2   3   4   5

    *Why did you give these ratings? What can be done to improve them?

Garage/Carport

22. Our transportation (*car, boats, motorcycle, motor home, bicycles, etc.*) is the best value possible.
Strongly disagree   Strongly agree
     1   2   3   4   5

23. All our vehicles are necessary.
Strongly disagree   Strongly agree
     1   2   3   4   5

   *Why did you give these ratings? What can be done to improve them?

Closets, Cabinets, Storage Spaces

24. Our family does not have things accumulated which are not being used (clothing, equipment, etc.).
Strongly disagree   Strongly agree
     1   2   3   4   5

25. Our storage is organized for efficient use.
Strongly disagree   Strongly agree
     1   2   3   4   5

26. Our family's hobby equipment expense is a reasonable use of money.
Strongly disagree   Strongly agree
     1   2   3   4   5

27. Our family members do not devote an excessive
    amount of time to hobbies.
    Strongly disagree   Strongly agree
        1   2   3   4   5

    *Why did you give these ratings? What can be done
     to improve them?

    If you find you have many unused things, perhaps
    your household should consider having a garage sale
    for God. Turn the items into cash and invest it in the
    Lord's work!

Yard

28. Our family does not spend excessively on maintenance
    of our yard (fertilizer, equipment, etc.).
    Strongly disagree   Strongly agree
        1   2   3   4   5

29. Family members do not spend excessive time
    maintaining our yard.
    Strongly disagree   Strongly agree
        1   2   3   4   5

30. Our yard is used as a gathering place for family, and
    Christian and non-Christian friends (cookouts, etc.)
    Strongly disagree   Strongly agree
        1   2   3   4   5

31. The appearance of our yard is a good testimony to our neighbors.
    Strongly disagree   Strongly agree
       1   2   3   4   5

*Why did you give these ratings? What can be done to improve them?

As you completed a room-by-room review of your possessions, if you did not review the media (books, television, radio, computer internet, etc.), do so now. In particular, ask yourself these questions:

Reading Matter (Books, Magazines, Newspapers)

32. The content of reading material in our home has a positive impact on our spiritual life:
    Strongly disagree   Strongly agree
       1   2   3   4   5

33. The content of reading material in our home has a positive impact on our family communications.
    Strongly disagree   Strongly agree
       1   2   3   4   5

34. Reading of the material in our home is a wise use of time.
    Strongly disagree   Strongly agree
       1   2   3   4   5

35. The money we spend on reading material in our home is a wise use of money.
    Strongly disagree   Strongly agree
          1   2   3   4   5

    *Why did you give these ratings? What can be done to improve them?

Television

The TV in the average American home is on thirty-three hours per week. Most children see more than 340,000 commercials before they graduate from high school. Rate your feelings about the use of the TV in your home.

36. Our family's viewing of television has a helpful impact on our spiritual life.
    Strongly disagree   Strongly agree
          1   2   3   4   5

37. Our family's viewing of television has a helpful impact on our moral values.
    Strongly disagree   Strongly agree
          1   2   3   4   5

    *Why or why not?

38. Our family's viewing of television has a helpful impact on our family's communications.
    Strongly disagree   Strongly agree
          1   2   3   4   5

*Why or why not?

39. Our family makes the best use of time when watching
    television.
    Strongly disagree   Strongly agree
        1   2   3   4   5

40. It would be helpful to have a weekly household council
    to discuss what programs will be viewed.
    Strongly disagree   Strongly agree
        1   2   3   4   5

    *Why did you give these ratings? What can be done
    to improve them?

Radios/CD/DVD Players/Tape Players

41. Our family spends the right amount of time listening to
    radios, CD/DVD, and/or tape players.
    Strongly disagree   Strongly agree
        1   2   3   4   5

42. Our family's listening to radios, CD/DVD and/or tape
    players have a helpful impact on moral values.
    Strongly disagree   Strongly agree
        1   2   3   4   5

    *Why or why not?

43. Our family's listening to radios, CD/DVD and/or tape players has a helpful impact on our family communications.

Strongly disagree   Strongly agree
    1   2   3   4   5

*Why or why not?

44. Our family's listening to radios, CD/DVD and/or tape players has a helpful impact on our spiritual development.

Strongly disagree   Strongly agree
    1   2   3   4   5

45. Our family makes wise use of money spent to purchase and maintain radios, CD/DVD and/or tape players, tapes, CDs/DVDs, etc.

Strongly disagree   Strongly agree
    1   2   3   4   5

*Why did you give these ratings? What can be done to improve them?

Future Legacy

Now take the opportunity to prayerfully consider all the Lord has given you—everything you have—your wealth, your possessions and belongings, even your family history and future legacy. Spend some time thinking of the disposition of these things after you are gone from this earth.

46. How does God want these things to be used when you are dead?

47. Have you made provision to pass along the physical and spiritual things in your life, which are most important?

48. Have you adequately provided for support of the Lord's work in your will?

For Reflection

If disaster was imminent and you could save only three things (not people) that you could carry, what would they be?

1.

2.

3.

Why would you save these three things?

The Future for Your Heirs

Christian values must be taught in the family. Possessions without proper values create problems. Parents must teach proper values by precept and example. If this is not done, children usually fight over the inheritance like buzzards over a carcass. Reflect on the following Scriptures.

1. Believers are to remember the LORD our God. Why?

> *You may say to yourself, "My power and the strength of my hands have produced this wealth for me." But remember the LORD your God, for it is he who gives you the ability to produce wealth, and so confirms his covenant, which he swore to your forefathers, as it is today.*[240]

2. Where do poverty and wealth come from?

> *The LORD sends poverty and wealth; he humbles and he exalts. He raises the poor from the dust and lifts the needy from the ash heap; he seats them with princes and has them inherit a throne of honor. For the foundations of the earth are the LORD's; upon them he has set the world.*[241]

3. How are we to honor the LORD?

> *Honor the LORD with your wealth.*[242]

---

[240] Deuteronomy 8:17-18
[241] 1 Samuel 2:7-8
[242] Proverbs 3:9

4. What will be important in day of wrath?

Wealth is worthless in the day of wrath, but righteousness delivers from death.[243]

5. What will happen to whoever trusts in riches?

Whoever trusts in his riches will fall, but the righteous will thrive like a green leaf.[244]

6. What is better than great wealth? Why?

Better a little with the fear of the LORD than great wealth with turmoil.[245]

7. Why does God give wealth?

Moreover, when God gives any man wealth and possessions, and enables him to enjoy them, to accept his lot and be happy in his work—this is a gift of God.[246]

8. What do the worries of this life and the deceitfulness of wealth do?

The one who received the seed that fell among the thorns is the man who hears the word, but the worries of this life and the deceitfulness of wealth

---

[243] Proverbs 11:4
[244] Proverbs 11:28
[245] Proverbs 15:16
[246] Ecclesiastes 5:19

choke it, making it unfruitful.[247]   *The seed that fell among thorns stands for those who hear, but as they go on their way they are choked by life's worries, riches and pleasures, and they do not mature.*[248]

9. When Jesus said to sell everything and give to the poor, why did the rich man become very sad?

When Jesus heard this, he said to him, "You still lack one thing. Sell everything you have and give to the poor, and you will have treasure in heaven. Then come, follow me." When he heard this, he became very sad, because he was a man of great wealth. Jesus looked at him and said, "How hard it is for the rich to enter the kingdom of God! Indeed, it is easier for a camel to go through the eye of a needle than for a rich man to enter the kingdom of God." Those who heard this asked, "Who then can be saved?" Jesus replied, "What is impossible with men is possible with God."[249]

10. What did Paul command Timothy to tell those who are rich in this present world?

Command those who are rich in this present world not to be arrogant nor to put their hope in wealth, which is so uncertain, but to put their hope in God, who richly provides us with everything for our enjoyment. Command them to do good, to be rich

---

[247] Matthew 13:22; Mark 4:19
[248] Luke 8:14
[249] Luke 18:22-27

in good deeds, and to be generous and willing to share.[250]

The word "house" is also used in Scripture to refer to the human body.

Now we know that if the earthly tent we live in is destroyed, we have a building from God, an eternal house in heaven, not built by human hands. Meanwhile we groan, longing to be clothed with our heavenly dwelling, because when we are clothed, we will not be found naked. For while we are in this tent, we groan and are burdened, because we do not wish to be unclothed but to be clothed with our heavenly dwelling, so that what is mortal may be swallowed up by life. Now it is God who has made us for this very purpose and has given us the Spirit as a deposit, guaranteeing what is to come. Therefore we are always confident and know that as long as we are at home in the body we are away from the Lord. We live by faith, not by sight. We are confident, I say, and would prefer to be away from the body and at home with the Lord. So we make it our goal to please him, whether we are at home in the body or away from it. For we must all appear before the judgment seat of Christ, that each one may receive what is due him for the things done while in the body, whether good or bad. Since, then, we know what it is to fear the Lord, we try to persuade men. What we are is plain to God, and I hope it is also plain to your conscience.[251]

---

[250] 1 Timothy 6:17-18
[251] 2 Corinthians 5:1-11

The Word became flesh and made his dwelling among us. We have seen his glory, the glory of the One and Only, who came from the Father, full of grace and truth.[252]

•••••

*Throughout the exercises in this *Appendix Three*, did you write your thoughts in a notebook? Writing helps you crystallize your thinking more accurately. If you have not done this, do so before you continue. You will be glad you did when you discuss this in your household council.

----

[252] John 1:14

Appendix Four

Suggested Service for Home Dedication

First, please be sure the family does a *Room-by-Room Review* and addresses what needs to be done as a result. A garage sale might be needed, or perhaps your will should be updated, etc. Your *Household Council* should meet to discuss issues that are raised through the review process.

When the family is ready, the following suggested service should be copied and studied by every member of the household so that it can be adapted to express the genuine beliefs and desires of all. Each person in the household should take one or more parts in the dedication service.

Opening Statement

> *Jesus said, "Here I am! I stand at the door and knock. If anyone hears my voice and opens the door, I will go in."*[253]

Opening Prayer

> God our Father, through faith in your Son, You make us members of your eternal family. You are the source and giver of love, which draws our earthly

---

[253] Revelation 3:20

families together. Be present with us in this home.
May your love enrich its fellowship, Your wisdom be
its guide, Your trust be its light, Your peace be its
benediction, through Jesus Christ, our Lord. Amen.

A Beatitude for the Family

Happy is the family that has a true home
Built by loyal hearts,
For home is not a dwelling but a living fellowship,
In love and understanding.
And happy is the family
Whose members find a deeper unity
In sharing truth and beauty and devotion to the good.
Their love shall be an altar fire
Burning in the temple of the Highest.

Selected Scripture Readings

*Whoever goes to the Lord for safety, whoever
remains under the protection of the Almighty, can say
to him, "You are my defender and protector. You are
my God; in you I trust."*[254]

*If the Lord does not build the house, the work of the
builders is useless.*[255]

*Lord, who may enter your Temple?
Who may worship on Zion, your sacred hill?*

---

[254] Psalm 91:1-2
[255] Psalm 127:1

A person who obeys in everything
And always does what is right,
Whose words are true and sincere,
And who does not slander others.
He does no wrong to his friends
And does not spread rumors about his neighbors.
He despises those whom God rejects,
But honors those who obey the Lord.
He always does what he promises,
No matter how much it may cost.
He makes loans without charging interest
And cannot be bribed to testify against the innocent.
Whoever does these things will always be secure.[256]

A new commandment I give you: love one another.
As I have loved you, so you must love one another.
All men will know that you are my disciples if you
love one another.[257]

Love is patient, love is kind. It does not envy, it does
not boast, it is not proud. It is not rude, it is not self-
seeking, it is not easily angered, it keeps no record of
wrongs. Love does not delight in evil but rejoices in
the truth. It always protects, always trusts, always
hopes, always perseveres.[258]

Love must be sincere. Hate what is evil; cling to
what is good. Be devoted to one another in brotherly
love. Honor one another above yourselves. Never be
lacking in zeal, but keep your spiritual fervor, serving

---

[256] Psalm 15:1-5
[257] John 13:34-35
[258] 1 Corinthians 13:4-7

the Lord. Be joyful in hope, patient in affliction, faithful in prayer. Share with God's people who are in need. Practice hospitality.[259]

Do not forget to entertain strangers, for by so doing some people have entertained angels without knowing it.[260]

When the Son of Man comes in his glory, and all the angels with him, he will sit on his throne in heavenly glory. All the nations will be gathered before him, and he will separate the people one from another as a shepherd separates the sheep from the goats. He will put the sheep on his right and the goats on his left. Then the King will say to those on his right, "Come, you who are blessed by my Father; take your inheritance, the kingdom prepared for you since the creation of the world. For I was hungry and you gave me something to eat, I was thirsty and you gave me something to drink, I was a stranger and you invited me in, I needed clothes and you clothed me, I was sick and you looked after me, I was in prison and you came to visit me." Then the righteous will answer him, "Lord, when did we see you hungry and feed you, or thirsty and give you something to drink? When did we see you a stranger and invite you in, or needing clothes and clothe you? When did we see you sick or in prison and go to visit you?" The King will reply, "I tell you the truth, whatever you did for one of the least of these brothers of mine, you did for me." Then he will say to those on his left, "Depart

---

[259] Romans 12:9-13
[260] Hebrews 13:2

from me, you who are cursed, into the eternal fire prepared for the devil and his angels. For I was hungry and you gave me nothing to eat, I was thirsty and you gave me nothing to drink, I was a stranger and you did not invite me in, I needed clothes and you did not clothe me, I was sick and in prison and you did not look after me." They also will answer, "Lord, when did we see you hungry or thirsty or a stranger or needing clothes or sick or in prison, and did not help you?" He will reply, "I tell you the truth, whatever you did not do for one of the least of these, you did not do for me." Then they will go away to eternal punishment, but the righteous to eternal life.[261]*

Do not let your hearts be troubled. Trust in God; trust also in me. In my Father's house are many rooms; if it were not so, I would have told you. I am going there to prepare a place for you. And if I go and prepare a place for you, I will come back and take you to be with me that you also may be where I am.[262]

Dedication and Candle-lighting Ceremony

Arrange seven small candles in a Jewish menorah or circle surrounding one larger candle. Before the ceremony begins, light the large candle, which represents Jesus. Each of the seven smaller candles, representing values you desire in your home, is then lit as the seven readings below are

---

[261] Matthew 25:31-46
[262] John 14:1-3

spoken. Light each smaller candle by lifting it to the larger candle and then place the smaller candle back in its position. The head of the household begins:

Jesus said, *"I am the Light of the world. He who follows Me shall not walk in darkness, but have the light of life."*[263]

We dedicate our home to love and understanding. May its joys and sorrows be shared and the individuality of each member appreciated. (Lift the first candle to the large candle. Light it and say the following.) We light a candle to family love. (Place the first candle back in its position.)

We dedicate our home to work and leisure. May it have gaiety and high fellowship, with kindness in its voices and laughter ringing within it walls. (Lift the first candle to the large candle. Light it and say the following.) We light a candle to happiness. (Place the first candle back in its position.)

We dedicate our home to friendly living. May its doors open in hospitality and its windows look out with kindness toward other homes. (Lift the first candle to the large candle. Light it and say the following.) We light a candle to friendship. (Place the first candle back in its position.)

We dedicate our home to cooperation. May its duties be performed in love, its furnishings bear witness that the work of others minister to our comfort, and its

---

[263] John 8:12

altar remind us that God works with us for supply of our daily needs. (Lift the first candle to the large candle. Light it and say the following.) We light a candle to cooperation. (Place the first candle back in its position.)

We dedicate our home to the appreciation of all things good and true. May the books bring wisdom, the pictures symbolize things beautiful, and the music bring joy and inspiration. (Lift the first candle to the large candle. Light it and say the following.) We light a candle to appreciation. (Place the first candle back in its position.)

We dedicate the time and talents of those who will live here to serve our generation and to help build a world in which every family may have a home of comfort and fellowship. (Lift the first candle to the large candle. Light it and say the following.) We light a candle to Christian service. (Place the first candle back in its position.)

We dedicate our home as a unit in the Church universal, an instrument of the Kingdom of God, a place for worship and Christian training and a threshold to life eternal. (Lift the first candle to the large candle. Light it and say the following.) We light a candle to spiritual enrichment. (Place the first candle back in its position.)

The household head closes this section by saying:
As the flames point upward, so our thoughts rise in gratitude to God for our home, and in prayer for His blessing in it.

Prayer of Dedication

Lord, bless this dwelling, not for any richness of material nor beauty of design, not for grace of furnishing, nor for loveliness of sight. For all these, we thank You. But especially bless this house because here is home; home in years of grave decision; home in springtime of life; home for all who weave the fabric of the family, the repeated tasks of days and labor to protect, enrich, train and fit the young; refuge for hard-pressed spirits and pain-filled bodies; a castle behind whose walls all may rest to go out refreshed to new achievement.

Let its doors be wide enough to welcome all friends. May the table have bread for all hungry mouths, the beds be hospitable to the weary, the books enable us to love the Lord with our minds. May our home be friendly and kind to every neighbor. Here let all gossip cease, all unworthy blame be left unspoken; here may gaiety and seriousness replace nervous haste, a sense of mission, relieve nagging lust for power. Here let the true, everlasting gospel embrace our family in undying bonds of love through Jesus Christ, our Lord. Amen

Song or Reading

Bless this house, O Lord, we pray,
Make it safe by night and day;
Bless these walls so firm and stout;
Keeping want and trouble out;
Bless the roof and chimney tall,
Let Thy peace lie over all;

Bless this door that it may prove
Ever open to joy and love.
Bless these windows shining bright,
Letting in God's heavenly light;
Bless the hearth a-blazing there;
With smoke ascending like a prayer;
Bless the folk who dwell within,
Keep them pure and free from sin;
Bless us all that we may be,
Fit, O Lord, to dwell with Thee.[264]

Benediction

The Lord bless us and keep us,
The Lord make His face to shine upon us
And be gracious unto us,
The Lord lift up His countenance upon us,
And give us peace, [265]
Both now and forever. Amen

•••••

[264] Helen Taylor, *Bless This House*, Boosey and Hawks, New York, NY, 1921.
[265] An adaptation of Numbers 6:24-26 KJV

Appendix Five

The Household Council For Improving Communications in Your Home

The Household Council is a special meeting of family members to discuss items of concern to the household. A good time to use these suggestions would be when the family meets to discuss the results of their Room-by-Room Review and individual inventory of possessions and lifestyle. The suggestions below might be helpful to this family communication process.

1. Begin with prayer.

2. Expect to gain new, positive insights into the people you may have lived with for many years!

3. Be prepared to have more than one discussion. Don't try to jam all the discussion into one, long session. It is better to have a number of brief sessions than to have one extended period. This is especially true if small children are involved.

4. Respect the differences of opinion others may have.

5. If there are disagreements, bring them to the Lord in prayer before the temperature of the discussion gets too warm.

6. When someone differs from you in his or her thinking, be sure you understand what is actually being said. Repeat the other person's words to be sure that you have accurately heard what you think the other person means. Once you understand the intent, then you can have a more meaningful discussion.

7. Let love rule through the entire discussion. Do not try to force your thinking as a legalistic, binding regulation on anyone else. Let the Spirit of God give a unity of heart and thought.

8. When you determine to implement some ministry, be specific as to who is responsible for what, and when this is to take place.

9. Don't remove something negative without replacing it with something positive, either physically or spiritually. *"When an evil spirit comes out of a man, it goes through arid places seeking rest and does not find it. Then it says, 'I will return to the house I left.' When it arrives, it finds the house unoccupied, swept clean and put in order. Then it goes and takes with it seven other spirits more wicked than itself, and they go in and live there. And the final condition of that man is worse than the first. That is how it will be with this wicked generation."*[266]

9. Conclude with prayer.

•••••

---

[266] Matthew 12:43-45

Appendix Six

Daily Prayer Guide Using the Westminster Shorter Catechism for Family Worship

Therefore you shall lay up these words of mine in your heart and in your soul, and bind them as a sign on your hand, and they shall be as frontlets between your eyes. You shall teach them to your children, speaking of them when you sit in your house, when you walk by the way, when you lie down, and when you rise up. And you shall write them on the doorposts of your house and on your gates, that your days and the days of your children may be multiplied in the land of which the LORD swore to your fathers to give them, like the days of the heavens above the earth.[267]

The Apostle Paul told his young disciple Timothy, *"Take heed to yourself and to the doctrine. Continue in them, for in doing this you will save both yourself and those who hear you."*[268]   To obey the Holy Spirit's words through Moses and Paul, try following Martin Luther's example of praying through a Catechism. If you do, you will find doctrine and devotion joined in your soul, like Siamese twins, connected at the heart.

---

[267] Deuteronomy 11:18-21
[268] 1 Timothy 4:16

We saw in *Improve Your Prayer Life*[269] that Luther's suggestions to his barber were based on the structure and content of his *Shorter Catechism*, which he prayerfully wrote and then, daily, prayed portions of until the day he died. Luther used the catechism, not as a textbook for doctrine, but as a daily resource for prayer. "Straightforwardly and clearly Luther described his own method, '*A Simple Way to Pray.*' He would take his Psalter to his room or, if there were church services that day, to the church and whisper to himself the memorized words of the catechism, elaborating each portion in a way to kindle a fire in his heart."[270] The guidelines below will help you follow Luther's example. The 107 questions, answers, and Scriptures of the *Westminster Shorter Catechism*[271] have been modernized into current English and arranged into a 90-day format.

There are so many varied situations in families, it would be impossible to provide one approach that would fit all homes. Below is one suggested way to pray together as a family using a catechism. We recommend, if at all possible, that this take about 10 minutes at the evening meal. Or, you might try getting the family up a few

---

[269] This is the first book in the Kingdom Campaign series. It is available from Serve International.

[270] Archie Parrish, *Improve Your Prayer Life,* Serve International, Atlanta, GA, 2000, p. 101.

[271] Many catechisms have been written for the instruction of believers. In addition to his *Shorter Catechism,* Luther wrote his *Larger Catechism.* Calvin also composed a brief catechism. The Westminster Divines penned both a *Shorter* and a *Larger Catechism.* Spurgeon modified the *Westminster Smaller Catechism* to comply with his Baptist beliefs. The *Heidelberg Catechism*, published by the Synod of Heidelberg, is unique because it was written in first person.

minutes earlier in the morning, so the family can sit down together.

If you are unable to see a way to worship together as a family, ask the Lord to help. The Bible makes it abundantly clear that regular family worship is essential for the family to accomplish God's purpose for it. God commands and promises, *"Call upon Me in the day of trouble; I will deliver you, and you shall glorify Me."*[272] If you see no way to establish regular family worship, that is a *"day of trouble"*! So *"call upon"* Him. He promises if you do that He *"will deliver you, and you shall glorify"* Him. His honor is at stake if you obediently call. He promises, *"I will instruct you and teach you in the way you should go; I will guide you with My eye."*[273]

If there are children under the age of six in the family, Marian M. Schoolland's book titled, *Leading Little Ones to God, A Child's Book of Bible Readings*[274] will be very helpful. This is a classic in its field, containing 86 daily devotionals for families with small children and step-by-step directions for the novice parent.

Newlyweds without children might find Charles and Norma Ellis' *Heirs Together of Life* to be beneficial. It contains a total of 274 daily devotions and Bible readings

---

[272] Psalm 50:15

[273] Psalm 32:8

[274] Marian M. Schoolland, *Leading Little Ones to God, A Child's Book of Bible Readings*, Wm. B. Eerdmans, Grand Rapids, MI, 1962. A classic in its field, this book contains 86 daily devotionals for families with small children, and step-by-step directions for the novice parent.

for husbands and wives, providing newlyweds a basic biblical foundation for their marriage.

One Way to Pray the Catechism as a Family

The head of the household, usually the husband, guides the members of the household through this Daily Prayer Guide. When the head of the family is unable to do this, the person upon whom this responsibility falls should take charge. Different family members can take turns reading aloud the passage from Psalms. All of the brief readings below come from Psalm 119, the theme of which is the word of God.

Next, the daily catechism questions and answers are read aloud. Family members should also read aloud Scripture passages relating to the answers. Together the family rephrases the answers in their own words, and then they discuss implications of the truth. As time allows, the leader shares relevant thoughts from journal entries made when studying *Improve Your Prayer Life* and *Intercede For and With Your Family.*

In the last few minutes, the leader moves the group to thank God for the truth, confess where they fall short, and ask His help. The leader then closes the time of family worship with prayer, placing the family in the hands of God.

Day 1:   Psalm 119:1-2
Question 1:   What is the chief end of man?
Answer: Man's chief end is to glorify God[a], and to enjoy him forever[b].
Scripture: [a]1 Corinthians 10:31, Romans 11:36
               [b]Psalm 73: 25-28

Day 2:   Psalm 119: 3-4
Question 2:   What rule has God given to direct us how we
                may glorify and enjoy him?
Answer: The word of God, which is contained in the
                scriptures of the Old and New Testaments[a], is
                the only rule to direct us how we may glorify
                and enjoy him[b].
Scripture: [a]2 Timothy 3:16
                [b]1 John 1:3-4

Day 3:   Psalm 119:5-6
Question 3:   What do the scriptures principally teach?
Answer: The scriptures principally teach what man is
                to believe concerning God, and what duty
                God requires of man[a].
Scripture: [b]2 Timothy 1:13 (See [a] in Question 2 above.)

Day 4:   Psalm 119:7-8
Question 4:   What is God?
Answer: God is a Spirit[a], infinite[b], eternal[c], and
                unchangeable[d], in his being[e], wisdom[f],
                power[g], holiness[h], justice, goodness, and
                truth.[i]
Scripture: [a]John 4:24
                [b]Job 11:7-9
                [c]Psalm 90:2
                [d]James 1:17
                [e]Exodus 3:14
                [f]Psalm 147:5
                [g]Revelation 4:8
                [h]Revelation 15:4
                [i]Exodus 34:6-7

Day 5:   Psalm 119:9-10
Question 5:   Are there more Gods than one?
Answer: There is but One only, the living and true
              God[a].
Scripture: [a]Deuteronomy 6:4; Jeremiah 10:10

Day 6:   Psalm 119:11-12
Question 6:   How many persons are there in the Godhead?
Answer: There are three persons in the Godhead; the
              Father, the Son, and the Holy Spirit; and
              these three are one God, the same in
              substance, equal in power and glory[a]
Scripture: [a]1 John 5:7; Matthew 28:19

Day 7:   Psalm 119:13-14
Question 7:   What are the decrees of God?
Answer: The decrees of God are, his eternal purpose,
              according to the counsel of his will,
              whereby, for his own glory, he has
              foreordained whatsoever comes to pass[a].
Scripture: [a]Ephesians 1:4,11; Romans 9:22-23

Day 8:   Psalm 119:15-16
Question 8:   How does God execute his decrees?
Answer: God executes his decrees in the works of
              creation and providence.
Scripture: Note: The Westminster Shorter Catechism
              contains no proof text for this question. It is
              suggested that Ephesians 1:11 be used for the
              day's devotions.

Day 9:   Psalm 119:17-18
Question 9:   What is the work of creation?
Answer: The work of creation is, God's making all
                things of nothing, by the word of his power,
                in the space of six days, and all very good[a].
Scripture: [a]Genesis 1 throughout; Hebrews 11:3

Day 10:   Psalm 119:19-20
Question 10:   How did God create man?
Answer: God created man male and female, after his
                own image, in knowledge, righteousness, and
                holiness, with dominion over the creatures[a].
Scripture: [a]Genesis 1:26-28; Colossians 3:10;
                Ephesians 4:24

Day 11:   Psalm 119:21-22
Question 11:   What are God's works of providence?
Answer: God's works of providence are, his most
                holy[a], wise[b], and powerful preserving[c] and
                governing all his creatures, and all their
                actions[d].
Scripture: [a]Psalm 145:17
                [b]Psalm 104:24; Isaiah 28:29
                [c]Hebrews 1:3
                [d]Psalm 103:19; Matthew 10:29-31

Day 12:   Psalm 119:23-24
Question 12: What special act of providence did God
              exercise toward man in the estate in which he
              was created?
Answer: When God had created man, he entered into a
              covenant of life with him, upon condition of
              perfect obedience; forbidding him to eat of
              the tree of the knowledge of good and evil,
              upon the pain of death[a].
Scripture: [a]Galatians 3:12; Genesis 2:17

Day 13:   Psalm 119:25-26
Question 13: Did our first parents continue in the estate
              in which they were created?
Answer: Our first parents, being left to the freedom of
              their own will, fell from the estate in which
              they were created, by sinning against God[a].
Scripture: [a]Genesis 3:6-8,13; Ecclesiastes 7:29

Day 14:   Psalm 119:27-28
Question 14: What is sin?
Answer: Sin is any want of conformity unto, or
              transgression of, the law of God[a].
Scripture: [a]1 John 3:4

Day 15:   Psalm 119:29-30
Question 15: What was the sin by which our first parents
             fell from the estate in which they were
             created?
Answer: The sin by which our first parents fell from
             the estate in which they were created, was
             their eating the forbidden fruit[a].
Scripture: [a]Genesis 3:6,12 (See [a] in Question 13
             above.)

Day 16:   Psalm 119:31-32
Question 16: Did all mankind fall in Adam's first
             transgression?
Answer: The covenant being made with Adam, not
             only for himself, but for his posterity; all
             mankind, descending from him by ordinary
             generation, sinned in him, and fell with him,
             in his first transgression[a].
Scripture: [a]Genesis 2:16-17; Romans 5:12;
             1 Corinthians 15:21-22

Day 17:   Psalm 119:33-34
Question 17: Into what estate did the fall bring mankind?
Answer: The fall brought mankind into an estate of sin
             and misery[a].
Scripture: [a]Romans 5:12

Day 18:   Psalm 119:35-36
Question 18: Wherein consists the sinfulness of that estate
                    into which man fell?
Answer: The sinfulness of that estate into which man
                    fell consists in the guilt of Adam's first sin,
                    the want of original righteousness, and the
                    corruption of his whole nature, which is
                    commonly called Original Sin; together with
                    all actual transgressions which proceed from
                    it[a].
Scripture: [a]Romans 5:10-20; Ephesians 2:1-3;
                    James 1:14-15; Matthew 15:19

Day 19:   Psalm 119:37-38
Question 19: What is the misery of that estate in which to
                    man fell?
Answer: All mankind by their fall lost communion
                    with God[a], are under his wrath and curse[b],
                    and so made liable to all miseries in this life,
                    to death itself, and to the pains of hell for
                    ever[c].
Scripture: [a]Genesis 3:8,10,24
                    [b]Ephesians 2:2-3; Galatians 3:10
                    [c]Lamentations 3:39; Romans 6:23;
                    Matthew 25:41,46

Day 20:   Psalm 119:39-40
Question 20:   Did God leave all mankind to perish in the
               estate of sin and misery?
Answer: God having, out of his mere good pleasure,
               from all eternity, elected some to everlasting
               life[a], did enter into a covenant of grace, to
               deliver them out of the estate of sin and
               misery, and to bring them into an estate of
               salvation by a Redeemer[b].
Scripture: [a]Ephesians 1:4;
               [b]Romans 3:20-22; Galatians 3:21-22

Day 21:   Psalm 119:41-42
Question 21:   Who is the Redeemer of God's elect?
Answer: The only Redeemer of God's elect is the
               Lord Jesus Christ[a], who, being the eternal
               Son of God, became man[b], and so was, and
               continues to be, God and man in two distinct
               natures, and one person, forever[c].
Scripture: [a]1 Timothy 2:5-6
               [b]John 1:14; Galatians 4:4
               [c]Romans 9:5; Luke 1:35; Colossians 2:9;
               Hebrews 7:24-25

Day 22:   Psalm 119:43-44
Question 22: How did Christ, being the Son of God,
              become man?
Answer: Christ, the Son of God, became man, by
              Taking to himself a true body[a], and a
              reasonable soul[b], being conceived by the
              power of the Holy Spirit, in the womb of the
              virgin Mary[c], and born of her, yet without
              sin[d].
Scripture: [a]Hebrews 2:14,16; Hebrews 10:5
              [b]Matthew 26:38
              [c]Luke 1:27,31,35,42
              [d]Galatians 4:4 (See [b] in Question 21 above.)

Day 23:   Psalm 119:45-46
Question 23: What offices does Christ execute as our
              Redeemer?
Answer: Christ, as our Redeemer, executes the offices
              of a prophet, of a priest, and of a king, both
              in his estate of humiliation and exaltation.[a]
Scripture: [a]Acts 3:21-22; Hebrews 12:25 compare with
              2 Corinthians 13:3; Hebrews 5:5-7;
              Hebrews 7:25; Psalm 2:6; Isaiah 9:6-7;
              Matthew 21:5; Psalm 2:8-11

Day 24:   Psalm 119:47-48
Question 24: How doth Christ execute the office of a
              prophet?
Answer: Christ executes the office of a prophet, in
              revealing to us, by his word and Spirit, the
              will of God for our salvation[a].
Scripture: [a]John 1:18; 1 Peter 1:10-12;
              John 15:15; John 20:31

Day 25:   Psalm 119:49-50
Question 25: How does Christ execute the office of a
              priest?
Answer: Christ executes the office of a priest, in his
              Once offering up of himself a sacrifice to
              satisfy divine justice[a], and reconcile us to
              God[b]; and in making continual intercession
              for us[c].
Scripture: [a]Hebrews 9:14,28
              [b]Hebrews 2:17
              [c]Hebrews 12:24-25

Day 26:   Psalm 119:51-52
Question 26: How does Christ execute the office of a king?
Answer: Christ executes the office of a king, in
              subduing us to himself[a], in ruling[b] and
              defending us[c], and in restraining and
              conquering all his and our enemies[d].
Scripture: [a]Acts 15:14-16
              [b]Isaiah 33:22
              [c]Isaiah 32:1-2
              [d]1 Corinthians 15:25; Psalm 110 throughout

Day 27:   Psalm 119:53-54
Question 27: In what did Christ's humiliation consist?
Answer: Christ's humiliation consisted in his being
                born, and that in a low condition[a], made
                under the law[b], undergoing the miseries of
                this life[c], the wrath of God[d], and the cursed
                death of the cross[e]; in being buried[f], and
                continuing under the power of death for a
                time[g].
Scripture: [a]Luke 2:7
                [b]Galatians 4:4
                [c]Hebrews 12:2-3; Isaiah 53:2-3
                [d]Luke 22:44; Matthew 27:46
                [e]Philippians 2:8
                [f]1 Corinthians 15:3-4
                [g]Acts 2:24-27,31

Day 28:   Psalm 119:55-56
Question 28: In what did the exaltation of Christ consist?
Answer: Christ's exaltation consists in his rising again
                from the dead on the third day[a], in ascending
                up into heaven[b], in sitting at the right hand of
                God the Father[c], and in coming to judge the
                world at the last day[d].
Scripture: [a]1 Corinthians 15:4
                [b]Mark 16:19
                [c]Ephesians 1:20
                [d]Acts 1:11; Acts 17:31

Day 29:   Psalm 119:57-58
Question 29: How are we made partakers of the
              redemption purchased by Christ?
Answer: We are made partakers of the redemption
              purchased by Christ, by the effectual
              application of it to us[a] by his Holy Spirit[b].
Scripture: [a]John 1:11-12
              [b]Titus 3:5-6

Day 30:   Psalm 119:59-60
Question 30: How does the Spirit apply to us the
              redemption purchased by Christ?
Answer: The Spirit applies to us the redemption
              Purchased by Christ, by working faith in us[a],
              and thereby uniting us to Christ in our
              effectual calling[b].
Scripture: [a]Ephesians 1:13-14; John 6:37,39;
              Ephesians 2:8
              [b]Ephesians 3:17; 1 Corinthians 1:9

Day 31:   Psalm 119:61-62

Question 31:   What is effectual calling?

Answer: Effectual calling is the work of God's Spirit[a], whereby, convincing us of our sin and misery[b], enlightening our minds in the knowledge of Christ[c], and renewing our wills[d], he doth persuade and enable us to embrace Jesus Christ, freely offered to us in the gospel[e].

Scripture: [a]2 Timothy 1:9; 2 Thessalonians 2:13-14
               [b]Acts 2:37
               [c]Acts 26:18
               [d]Ezekiel 36:26-27
               [e]John 6:44-45; Philippians 2:13

Day 32:   Psalm 119:63-64

Question 32:   What benefits do they that are effectually called partake of in this life?

Answer: They that are effectually called do in this life partake of justification[a], adoption[b], and sanctification, and the several benefits which in this life do either accompany or flow from them[c].

Scripture: [a]Romans 8:30
               [b]Ephesians 1:5
               [c]1 Corinthians 1:26,30

Day 33: Psalm 119:65-66
Question 33: What is justification?
Answer: Justification is an act of God's free grace,
in which he pardons all our sins[a], and accepts
us as righteous in his sight[b], only for the
righteousness of Christ imputed to us[c], and
received by faith alone[d].
Scripture: [a]Romans 3:24-25; Romans 4:6-8
[b]2 Corinthians 5:19,21
[c]Romans 5:17-19
[d]Galatians 2:16; Philippians 3:9

Day 34: Psalm 119:67-68
Question 34: What is adoption?
Answer: Adoption is an act of God's free grace[a],
whereby we are received into the number,
and have a right to all the privileges of the
sons of God[b].
Scripture: [a]1 John 3:1
[b]John 1:12; Romans 8:17

Day 35: Psalm 119:69-70
Question 35: What is sanctification?
Answer: Sanctification is the work of God's free
grace[a], whereby we are renewed in the whole
man after the image of God[b], and are enabled
more and more to die unto sin, and live unto
righteousness[c].
Scripture: [a]2 Thessalonians 2:13
[b]Ephesians 4:23-24
[c]Romans 6:4,6; Romans 8:1

Day 36:   Psalm 119:71-72
Question 36: What are the benefits which in this life
               accompany or flow from justification,
               adoption, and sanctification?
Answer: The benefits which in this life accompany
               or flow from justification, adoption, and
               sanctification, are, assurance of God's love,
               peace of conscience[a], joy in the Holy Spirit[b],
               increase of grace[c], and perseverance therein
               to the end[d].
Scripture: [a]Romans 5:1-2,5
               [b]Romans 14:17
               [c]Proverbs 4:18
               [d]1 John 5:13; 1 Peter 1:5

Day 37:   Psalm 119:73-74
Question 37: What benefits do believers receive from
               Christ at death?
Answer: The souls of believers are at their death made
               perfect in holiness[a], and do immediately pass
               into glory[b]; and their bodies, being still
               united to Christ[c], do rest in their graves[d] till
               the resurrection[e].
Scripture: [a]Hebrews 12:28
               [b]2 Corinthians 5:1,6,8; Philippians 1:23;
               Luke 23:43
               [c]1 Thessalonians 4:14
               [d]Isaiah 57:2
               [e]Job 19:26-27

Day 38:   Psalm 119:75-76
Question 38: What benefits do believers receive from Christ at the resurrection?
Answer: At the resurrection, believers being raised up in glory[a], shall be openly acknowledged and acquitted in the day of judgment[b], and made perfectly blessed in the full enjoying of God[c] to all eternity[d].
Scripture: [a]1 Corinthians 15:43
          [b]Matthew 25:23; Matthew 10:32
          [c]1 John 3:2; 1 Corinthians 13:12
          [d]1 Thessalonians 4:17

Day 39:   Psalm 119:77-78
Question 39: What is the duty which God requires of man?
Answer: The duty which God requires of man, is obedience to his revealed will[a].
Scripture: Micah 6:8; 1 Samuel 15:22

Day 40:   Psalm 119:79-80
Question 40: What did God at first reveal to man for the rule of his obedience?
Answer: The rule which God at first revealed to man for his obedience, was the moral law[a].
Scripture: [a]Romans 2:14-15; Romans 10:5

Day 41:   Psalm 119:81-82
Question 41: Where is the moral law summarily comprehended?
Answer: The moral law is summarily comprehended in the ten commandments[a].
Scripture: [a]Deuteronomy 10:4; Matthew 19:17

Day 42:   Psalm 119:83-84
Question 42: What is the sum of the ten commandments?
Answer: The sum of the ten commandments is, to love
             the Lord our God with all our heart, with all
             our soul, with all our strength, and with all
             our mind; and our neighbors as ourselves[a].
Scripture: [a]Matthew 22:37-40

Day 43:   Psalm 119:85-86
Question 43: What is the preface to the ten
             commandments?
Answer: The preface to the ten commandments is in
             these words, *"I am the Lord your God, who
             brought you out of the land of Egypt, out of
             the house of bondage."*[a]
Scripture: [a]Exodus 20:2

Day 44:   Psalm 119:87-88
Question 44: What does the preface to the ten
             commandments teach us?
Answer: The preface to the ten commandments
             teaches us, that because God is the Lord, and
             our God, and Redeemer, therefore we are
             bound to keep all his commandments[a].
Scripture: [a]Luke 1:74-75; 1 Peter 1:15-19

Day 45:   Psalm 119:89-90
Question 45: Which is the first commandment?
Answer: The first commandment is, *"You shall have*
             no other gods before Me."[a]
Scripture: [a]Exodus 20:3

Day 46:   Psalm 119:91-92
Question 46: What is required in the first commandment?
Answer: The first commandment requires us to know
             and acknowledge God to be the only true
             God, and our God[a], and to worship and
             glorify him accordingly[b].
Scripture: [a]1 Chronicles 28:9; Deuteronomy 26:17
             [b]Matthew 4:10; Psalm 29:2

Day 47:   Psalm 119:93-94
Question 47: What is forbidden in the first commandment?
Answer: The first commandment forbids the denying[a],
             or not worshipping and glorifying the true
             God as God[b], and our God[c]; and the giving of
             that worship and glory to any other, which is
             due to him alone[d].
Scripture: [a]Psalm 14:1
             [b]Romans 1:21
             [c]Psalm 81:10-11
             [d]Romans 1:25

<u>Day 48</u>: Psalm 119:95-96

Question 48: What are we specially taught by these words *before me* in the first commandment?

Answer: These words *before me* in the first commandment teach us, that God, who sees all things, takes notice of, and is much displeased with, the sin of having any other god[a].

Scripture: [a]Ezekiel 8:5-6; Psalm 96:20-21

<u>Day 49</u>: Psalm 119:97-98

Question 49: Which is the second commandment?

Answer: The second commandment is, *"You shall not make for yourself a carved image, or any likeness of anything that is in heaven above, or that is in the earth beneath, or that is in the water under the earth; you shall not bow down to them nor serve them. For I, the Lord your God, am a jealous God, visiting the iniquity of the fathers on the children to the third and fourth generations of those who hate Me, but showing mercy to thousands, to those who love Me and keep My commandments.*"[a]

Scripture: [a]Exodus 20:4-6

Day 50:   Psalm 119:99-100
Question 50: What is required in the second
              commandment?
Answer: The second commandment requires the
              receiving, observing, and keeping pure and
              entire, all such religious worship and
              ordinances as God had appointed in his
              word[a].
Scripture: [a]Deuteronomy 32:46; Matthew 28:20;
              Acts 2:42

Day 51:   Psalm 119:101-102
Question 51: What is forbidden in the second
              commandment?
Answer: The second commandment forbids the
              worshipping of God by images[a], or any other
              way not appointed in his word[b].
Scripture: [a]Deuteronomy 4:15-19; Exodus 32:5,8
              [b]Deuteronomy 12:31-32

Day 52:   Psalm 119:103-104
Question 52: What are the reasons annexed to the second
              commandment?
Answer: The reasons annexed to the second
              commandment are, God's sovereignty over
              us[a], his propriety in us[b], and the zeal he has
              to his own worship[c].
Scripture: [a]Psalm 95:2-3,6
              [b]Psalm 45:11
              [c]Exodus 34:13-14

Day 53:   Psalm 119:105-106
Question 53: Which is the third commandment?
Answer: The third commandment is, *"You shall not take the name of the Lord your God in vain, for the Lord will not hold him guiltless who takes his name in vain."*[a]
Scripture: [a]Exodus 20:7

Day 54:   Psalm 119:107-108
Question 54: What is required in the third commandment?
Answer: The third commandment requires the holy and reverent use of God's names[a], titles[b], attributes[c], ordinances[d], word[e] and works[f].
Scripture: [a]Matthew 6:9; Deuteronomy 28:58
              [b]Psalm 68:4
              [c]Revelation 15:3-4
              [d]Malachi 1:11,14
              [e]Psalm 138:1-2
              [f]Job 36:24

Day 55:   Psalm 119:109-110
Question 55: What is forbidden in the third commandment?
Answer: The third commandment forbids all profaning or abusing of any thing by which God makes himself known[a].
Scripture: [a]Malachi 1:6-7,12; Malachi 2:2; Malachi 3:14

Day 56:   Psalm 119:111-112
Question 56:   What is the reason annexed to the third
               commandment?
Answer: The reason annexed to the third
               commandment is, that however the breakers
               of this commandment may escape
               punishment from men, yet the Lord our God
               will not suffer them to escape his righteous
               judgment[a].
Scripture: [a]1 Samuel 2:12,17,22,29; 1 Samuel 3:13;
               Deuteronomy 28:58-59

Day 57:   Psalm 119:113-114
Question 57:   Which is the fourth commandment?
Answer: The fourth commandment is, *"Remember the*
               Sabbath day, to keep it holy. Six days you
               shall labor and do all your work, but the
               seventh day is the Sabbath of the Lord your
               God. In it you shall do no work: you, nor
               your son, nor your daughter, nor your male
               servant, nor your female servant, nor your
               cattle, nor your stranger who is within your
               gates. For in six days the Lord made the
               heavens and the earth, the sea, and all that is
               in them, and rested the seventh day.
               Therefore the Lord blessed the Sabbath day
               and hallowed it."[a]
Scripture: [a]Exodus 20:8-11

Day 58:   Psalm 119:115-116
Question 58: What is required in the fourth
              commandment?
Answer: The fourth commandment requires the
              keeping holy to God such set times as he has
              appointed in his Word; expressly one whole
              day in seven, to be a holy Sabbath to
              himself[a].
Scripture: [a]Deuteronomy 5:12-14

Day 59:   Psalm 119:117-118
Question 59: Which day of the seven has God appointed to
              be the weekly Sabbath?
Answer: From the beginning of the world to the
              resurrection of Christ, God appointed the
              seventh day of the week to be the weekly
              Sabbath; and the first day of the week ever
              since, to continue to the end of the world,
              which is the Christian Sabbath[a].
Scripture: [a]Genesis 2:2-3; 1 Corinthians 16:1-2;
              Acts 20:7

Day 60:   Psalm 119:119-120
Question 60:   How is the Sabbath to be sanctified?
Answer: The Sabbath is to be sanctified by a holy
               resting all that day[a], even from such worldly
               employments and recreations as are lawful on
               other days[b]; and spending the whole time in
               the public and private exercises of God's
               worship[c], except so much as is to be taken up
               in the works of necessity and mercy[d].
Scripture: [a]Exodus 20:8,10; Exodus 16:25-28
               [b]Nehemiah 13:15-22
               [c]Luke 4:16; Acts 20:7 (See [a] in Question 59
               above.); Psalm 92:title; Isaiah 66:23
               [d]Matthew 12:1-31

Day 61:   Psalm 119:121-122
Question 61:   What is forbidden in the fourth
               commandment?
Answer: The fourth commandment forbids the
               omission or careless performance of the
               duties required[a], and the profaning the day by
               idleness[b], or doing that which is in itself
               sinful[c], or by unnecessary thoughts, words, or
               works about our worldly employments or
               recreations[d].
Scripture: [a]Ezekiel 22:26; Amos 8:5; Malachi 1:13
               [b]Acts 20:7,9
               [c]Ezekiel 23:38
               [d]Jeremiah 17:24-26; Isaiah 58:13

Day 62:   Psalm 119:123-124
Question 62: What are the reasons annexed to the fourth commandment?
Answer: The reasons annexed to the fourth commandment are, God's allowing us six days of the week for our own employments[a], his challenging a special propriety in the seventh, his own example, and his blessing the Sabbath day[b].
Scripture: [a]Exodus 20:9
               [b]Exodus 20:11

Day 63:   Psalm 119:125-126
Question 63: Which is the fifth commandment?
Answer: The fifth commandment is, *"Honor your father and your mother, that your days may be long upon the land which the Lord your God is giving you."*[a]
Scripture: [a]Exodus 20:12

Day 64:   Psalm 119:127-128
Question 64: What is required in the fifth commandment?
Answer: The fifth commandment requires the preserving the honor, and performing the duties, belonging to every one in their several places and relations, as superiors[a], inferiors[b] or equals[c].
Scripture: [a]Ephesians 5:21
               [b]1 Peter 2:17
               [c]Romans 12:10

Day 65:   Psalm 119:129-130
Question :   What is forbidden in the fifth commandment?
Answer: The fifth commandment forbids the
                neglecting of, or doing any thing against, the
                honor and duty which belongs to every one
                in their several places and relations[a].
Scripture: [a]Matthew 15:46; Ezekiel 34:2-4;
                Romans 13:8

Day 66:   Psalm 119:131-132
Question 66:   What is the reason annexed to the fifth
                commandment?
Answer: The reason annexed to the fifth
                commandment, is a promise of long life and
                prosperity (as far as it shall serve for God's
                glory and their own good) to all such as keep
                this commandment[a].
Scripture: [a]Deuteronomy 5:16; Ephesians 6:2-3

Day 67:   Psalm 119:133-134
Question 67:   Which is the sixth commandment?
Answer: The sixth commandment is, *"You shall not
                murder."*[a]
Scripture: [b]Exodus 20:13

Day 68:   Psalm 119:135-136
Question 68:   What is required in the sixth commandment?
Answer: The sixth commandment requires all lawful
                endeavors to preserve our own life[a], and the
                life of others[b].
Scripture: [a]Ephesians 5:28-29
                [d]1 Kings 18:4

Day 69:   Psalm 119:137-138
Question 69: What is forbidden in the sixth
              commandment?
Answer: The sixth commandment forbids the taking
              away of our own life, or the life of our
              neighbor unjustly, or whatever tends toward
              that[a].
Scripture: [a]Acts 16:28

Day 70:   Psalm 119:139-140
Question 70: Which is the seventh commandment?
Answer: The seventh commandment is, *"You shall not
              commit adultery."*[a]
Scripture: [a]Exodus 20:14

Day 71:   Psalm 119:141-142
Question 71: What is required in the seventh
              commandment?
Answer: The seventh commandment requires the
              preservation of our own and our neighbor's
              chastity, in heart, speech, and behavior[a].
Scripture: [a]1 Corinthians 7:2-3,5,34,36; Colossians 4:6;
              1 Peter 3:2

Day 72:   Psalm 119:143-144
Question 72: What is forbidden in the seventh
              commandment?
Answer: The seventh commandment forbids all
              unchaste thoughts, words, and actions[a].
Scripture: [a]Matthew 15:19; Matthew 5:28;
              Ephesians 5:3-4

Day 73:   Psalm 119:145-146
Question 73: Which is the eighth commandment?
Answer: The eighth commandment is, *"You shall not steal."*[a]
Scripture: [a]Exodus 20:15
Question 74: What is required in the eighth commandment?
Answer: The eighth commandment requires the lawful procuring and furthering the wealth and outward estate of ourselves and others[a].
Scripture: [a]Genesis 30:30; 1 Timothy 5:8; Leviticus 25:35; Deuteronomy 22:1-5; Exodus 23:4-5; Genesis 47:14,20

Day 74:   Psalm 119:147-148
Question 75: What is forbidden in the eighth commandment?
Answer: The eighth commandment forbids whatsoever does or may unjustly hinder our own or our neighbor's wealth or outward estate[a].
Scripture: [a]Proverbs 21:17; Proverbs 23:20-21; Proverbs 28:19; Ephesians 4:28
Question 76: Which is the ninth commandment?
Answer: The ninth commandment is, *"You shall not bear false witness against your neighbor."*[a]
Scripture: [a]Exodus 20:16

Day 75:   Psalm 119:149-150
Question 77: What is required in the ninth commandment?
Answer: The ninth commandment requires the
             maintaining and promoting of truth between
             man and man[a], and of our own and our
             neighbor's good name[b], especially in
             witness-bearing[c].
Scripture: [a]Zechariah 8:16
             [b]3 John 12
             [c]Proverbs 14:5,25
Question 78 What is forbidden in the ninth
             commandment?
Answer: The ninth commandment forbids whatsoever
             is prejudicial to truth, or injurious to our own
             or our neighbor's good name[a].
Scripture: [a]1 Samuel 17:28

Day 76:   Psalm 119:151-152
Question 79: Which is the tenth commandment?
Answer: The tenth commandment is, *"You shall not
             covet your neighbor's house; you shall not
             covet your neighbor's wife, nor his male
             servant, nor his female servant, nor his ox,
             nor his donkey, nor anything that is your
             neighbor's."*[a]
Scripture: [a]Exodus 20:17
Question 80 What is required in the tenth commandment?
Answer: The tenth commandment requires full
             contentment with our own condition[a], with a
             right and charitable frame of spirit toward our
             neighbor, and all that is his[b].
Scripture: [a]Hebrews 13:5; 1 Timothy 6:6
             [b]Job 31:29; Romans 12:15; 1 Timothy 1:5;
             1 Corinthians 13:4-7

Day 77:   Psalm 119:153-154

Question 81: What is forbidden in the tenth commandment?

Answer: The tenth commandment forbids all discontentment with our own estate[v], envying or grieving at the good of our neighbor[w], and all inordinate emotions and affections to any thing that is his[x].

Scripture: [a]1 Kings 21:4; Esther 5:13; 1 Corinthians 10:10
[b]Galatians 5:26; James 3:14,16
[c]Romans 7:7-8; Romans 13:9; Deuteronomy 5:21

Question 82 Is any man able perfectly to keep the commandments of God?

Answer: No mere man since the fall is able in this life perfectly to keep the commandments of God[a], but does daily break them in thought, word, and deed[b].

Scripture: [a]Ecclesiastes 7:20; 1 John 1:8,10; Galatians 5:17
[b]Genesis 6:5; Genesis 8:21; Romans 3:9-21; James 3:2-13

<u>Day 78:</u>   Psalm 119:155-156
Question 83: Are all transgressions of the law equally
                   heinous?
Answer: Some sins in themselves, and by reason of
                   several aggravations, are more heinous in the
                   sight of God than others[a].
Scripture: [a]Ezekiel. 8:6,13,15; 1 John 5:16;
                   Psalm 78:17,32,56
Question 84: What does every sin deserve?
Answer: Every sin deserves God's wrath and curse,
                   both in this life, and that which is to come[a].
                   [a]Ephesians 5:6; Galatians 3:10;
                   Lamentations 3:39; Matthew 25:41

<u>Day 79:</u>   Psalm 119:157-158
Question 85: What does God require of us, that we may
                   escape his wrath and curse due to us for sin?
Answer: To escape the wrath and curse of God due to
                   us for sin, God requires of us faith in Jesus
                   Christ, repentance unto life[a], with the diligent
                   use of all the outward means by which Christ
                   communicates to us the benefits of
                   redemption[b].
Scripture: [a]Acts 20:21
                   [b]Proverbs 2:1-5; Proverbs 8:33-36;
                   Isaiah 55:3
Question 86 What is faith in Jesus Christ?
Answer: Faith in Jesus Christ is a saving grace[a],
                   whereby we receive and rest upon him alone
                   for salvation, as he is offered to us in the
                   gospel[b].
Scripture: [a]Hebrews 10:39
                   [b]John 1:12; Isaiah 26:3-4; Philippians 3:9;
                   Galatians 2:16

Day 80:   Psalm 119:159-160
Question 87: What is repentance unto life?
Answer: Repentance unto life is a saving grace[a],
                        whereby a sinner, out of a true sense of his
                        sin[b], and apprehension of the mercy of God
                        in Christ[c], does, with grief and hatred of his
                        sin, turn from it unto God[d], with full purpose
                        of, and endeavor after, new obedience[e].
Scripture: [a]Acts 11:18
                        [b]Acts 2:37-38
                        [c]Joel 2:12; Jeremiah 3:22
                        [d]Jeremiah 31:18-19; Ezekiel 36:31
                        [e]2 Corinthians 7:11
Question 88: What are the outward means by which Christ
                        communicates to us the benefits of
                        redemption?
Answer: The outward and ordinary means whereby
                        Christ communicates to us the benefits of
                        redemption, are his ordinances, especially the
                        word, sacraments, and prayer; all which are
                        made effectual to the elect for salvation[a].
Scripture: [a]Matthew 28:19-20; Acts 2:42,46-47

Day 81:   Psalm 119:161-162
Question 89: How is the word made effectual to salvation?
Answer: The Spirit of God makes the reading, but
              especially the preaching of the word, an
              effectual means of convincing and converting
              sinners, and of building them up in holiness
              and comfort, through faith, unto salvation[a].
Scripture: [a]Nehemiah 8:8; 1 Corinthians 14:24-25;
              Acts 26:18; Psalm 19:8; Acts 20:32;
              Romans 15:4; 2 Timothy 3:15-17;
              Romans 10:13-17; Romans 1:16
Question 90   How is the word to be read and heard, that it
              may become effectual to salvation?
Answer: That the word may become effectual to
              salvation, we must attend thereunto with
              diligence[a], preparation[b], and prayer[c]; receive
              it with faith and love[d], lay it up in our hearts[e],
              and practice it in our lives[f].
Scripture: [a]Proverbs 8:34
              [b]1 Peter 2:1-2
              [c]Psalm 119:18
              [d]Hebrews 4:2; 2 Thessalonians 2:10
              [e]Psalm 119:11
              [f]Luke 8:15; James 1:25

Day 82:   Psalm 119:163-164

Question 91: How do the sacraments become effectual means of salvation?

Answer: The sacraments become effectual means of salvation, not from any virtue in them, or in him that administers them; but only by the blessing of Christ[a], and the working of his Spirit in them that by faith receive them[b].

Scripture: [a]1 Peter 3:21; Matthew 3:11; 1 Corinthians 3:6-7
[b]1 Corinthians 12:13

Question 92: What is a sacrament?

Answer: A sacrament is an holy ordinance instituted by Christ; in which, by sensible signs, Christ, and the benefits of the new covenant, are represented, sealed, and applied to believers[a].

Scripture: [a]Genesis 17:7,10; Exodus 12; 1 Corinthians 11:23,26

Day 83:   Psalm 119:165-166

Question 93: Which are the sacraments of the New Testament?

Answer: The sacraments of the New Testament are, baptism[a], and the Lord's Supper[b].

Scripture: [a]Matthew 28:19
            [b]Matthew 26:26-28

Question 94: What is baptism?

Answer: Baptism is a sacrament, in which the washing with water in the name of the Father, and of the Son, and of the Holy Ghost[a], signifies and seals our ingrafting into Christ, and the partaking of the benefits of the covenant of grace, and our engagement to be the Lord's[b].

Scripture: [a]Matthew 28:19 (See [a] in Question 93 above.)
            [b]Romans 6:4; Galatians 3:27

Day 84:   Psalm 119:167-168

Question 95: To whom is baptism to be administered?

Answer: Baptism is not to be administered to any that are out of the visible church, till they profess their faith in Christ, and obedience to him[a]; but the infants of such as are members of the visible church are to be baptized[b].

Scripture: [a]Acts 8:36-37; Acts 2:38
[b]Acts 2:38-39 (See [a] above.); Genesis 17:10 (See [a] in Questions 92 above.) compared with Colossians 2:11-12; 1 Corinthians 7:14

Question 96: What is the Lord's Supper?

Answer: The Lord's Supper is a sacrament, in which, by giving and receiving bread and wine, according to Christ's appointment, his death is shown forth; and the worthy receivers are, not after a corporal and carnal manner, but by faith, made partakers of his body and blood, with all his benefits, to their spiritual nourishment, and growth in grace[a].

Scripture: [a]1 Corinthians 11:23-26; 1 Corinthians 10:16

Day 85:   Psalm 119:169-170

Question 97: What is required to the worthy receiving of
              the Lord's Supper?

Answer: It is required of them that would worthily
              partake of the Lord's Supper, that they
              examine themselves of their knowledge to
              discern the Lord's body[a], of their faith to feed
              upon him[b], of their repentance[c], love[d], and
              new obedience[e]; lest, coming unworthily,
              they eat and drink judgment to themselves[f].

Scripture: [a]1 Corinthians 11:28-29
              [b]2 Corinthians 13:5
              [c]1 Corinthians 11:31
              [d]1 Corinthians 10:16-17
              [e]1 Corinthians 5:7-8
              [f]1 Corinthians 11:28-29 (See [a] above.)

Question 98: What is prayer?

Answer: Prayer is an offering up of our desires unto
              God[a], for things agreeable to his will[b], in the
              name of Christ[c], with confession of our sins[d],
              and thankful acknowledgment of his
              mercies[e].

Scripture: [a]Psalm 62:8
              [b]1 John 5:14
              [c]John 16:23
              [d]Psalm 32:5-6; Daniel 9:4
              [e]Philippians 4:6

Day 86:   Psalm 119:171-172
Question 99:   What rule has God given for our direction in prayer?
Answer: The whole word of God is of use to direct us in prayer[a]; but the special rule of direction is that form of prayer which Christ taught his disciples, commonly called The Lord's Prayer[b].
Scripture: [a]1 John 5:14
               [b]Matthew 6:9-13 compared with Luke 11:2-4
Question 100:What does the preface of the Lord's Prayer teach us?
Answer: The preface of the Lord's Prayer (which is, *Our Father in heaven*[a]) teaches us to draw near to God with all holy reverence and confidence, as children to a father, able and ready to help us[b]; and that we should pray with and for others[c].
Scripture: [a]Matthew 6:9
               [b]Romans 8:15; Luke 11:13
               [c]Acts 12:5; 1 Timothy 2:1-2

Day 87:   Psalm 119:173

Question 101: What do we pray for in the first petition?

Answer: In the first petition (which is, *Hallowed be Your name*[a]) we pray, that God would enable us and others to glorify him in all that whereby he makes himself known[b]; and that he would dispose all things to his own glory[c].

Scripture: [a]Matthew 6:9
               [b]Psalm 67:2-3
               [c]Psalm 83

Question 102: What do we pray for in the second petition?

Answer: In the second petition (which is, *Your kingdom come*[a]) we pray, that Satan's kingdom may be destroyed[b]; and that the kingdom of grace may be advanced[c], ourselves and others brought into it, and kept in it[d]; and that the kingdom of glory may be hastened[e].
               [a]Matthew 6:10
               [b]Psalm 68:1,18
               [c]Revelation 12:10-11
               [d]2 Thessalonians 3:1; Romans 10:1; John 17:9,20
               [e]Revelation 22:20

216

Day 88:   Psalm 119: 174
Question 103:What do we pray for in the third petition?
Answer: In the third petition (which is, *Your will be
               done, on earth as it is in heaven*[a]) we pray,
               that God, by his grace, would make us able
               and willing to know, obey, and submit to his
               will in all things[b], as the angels do in
               heaven[c].
Scripture: [a]Matthew 6:10
               [b]Psalm 67; Psalm 119:36; Matthew 26:39;
               2 Samuel 15:25; Job 1:21
               [c]Psalm 103:20-21
Question 104:What do we pray for in the fourth petition?
Answer: In the fourth petition (which is, *Give us this
               day our daily bread*[a]) we pray, that of God's
               free gift we may receive a competent portion
               of the good things of this life, and enjoy his
               blessing with them[b].
Scripture: [a]Matthew 6:11
               [b]Proverbs 30:8-9; Genesis 28:20;
               1 Timothy 4:4-5

Day 89:   Psalm 119:175

Question 105:What do we pray for in the fifth petition?

Answer: In the fifth petition (which is, *And forgive us our debts, as we forgive our debtors*[a]) we pray, that God, for Christ's sake, would freely pardon all our sins[b]; which we are the rather encouraged to ask, because by his grace we are enabled from the heart to forgive others[c].

Scripture: [a]Matthew 6:12
              [b]Psalm 51:1-2,7,9; Daniel 9:17-19
              [c]Luke 11:4; Matthew 18:35

Question 106:What do we pray for in the sixth petition?

Answer: In the sixth petition (which is, *And do not lead us into temptation, but deliver us from the evil one*[a]) we pray, that God would either keep us from being tempted to sin[b], or support and deliver us when we are tempted[c].

Scripture: [a]Matthew 6:13
              [b]Matthew 26:41
              [c]2 Corinthians 12:7-8

Day 90:   Psalm 119:176
Question 107:What does the conclusion of the Lord's
                 prayer teach us?
Answer: The conclusion of the Lord's Prayer (which
                 is, *For Yours is the kingdom and the power
                 and the glory forever. Amen.*[a]) teaches us to
                 take our encouragement in prayer from God
                 only[b], and in our prayers to praise him,
                 ascribing kingdom, power, and glory to
                 him[c]. And, in testimony of our desire, and
                 assurance to be heard, we say, Amen[d].
Scripture: [a]Matthew 6:13
                 [b]Daniel 9:4,7-9,16-19
                 [c]1 Chronicles 29:10-13
                 [d]1 Corinthians 14:16; Revelation 22:20-21

•••••

Selected Bibliography

1. *As for my House, A Father's Guide for Fruitful Family Worship*, Great Commission Publications, Suwanee, GA.
2. *Catechism for Young Children, An Introduction to the Shorter Catechism*, Original Edition, Christian Education and Publications, Atlanta, GA.
3. Colson, Charles, *How Now Shall We Live?*, Tyndale Publishers, Carol Stream, IL, 1999.
4. Ellis, Charles and Norma, *Heirs Together of Life, Daily Bible Readings for Husbands and Wives*, The Banner of Truth Trust, Carlisle, PA, 1980.
5. *First Catechism, Biblical Truth for God's Children, Based on the Catechism for Young Children, An Introduction to the Shorter Catechism*, Great Commission Publications, Atlanta, GA, 1996.
6. Foster, Richard J., "Sex," Part II, pages 91-171, *The Challenge of the Disciplined Life, Christian Reflections on Money, Sex, & Power*, HarperColins, San Francisco, CA, 1985
7. Howard, Thomas, *Hallowed Be This House*, 2nd Edition, Ignatius Press, San Francisco, CA, 1989.
8. Horton, Joyce, *How to Teach the Catechism to Children*, Campus Christian Bookstore, Reformed Theological Seminary, Jackson, MS, 1979.
9. Jay, William, *Morning Exercises for Every Day in the Year*, Sprinkle Publications, Harrisburg, VA, 1998.

10. Jay, William, *Evening Exercises for Every Day in the Year*, Sprinkle Publications, Harrisburg, VA, 1998.
11. Johnson, Terry, *The Family Worship Book*, Christian Focus Publications, Fearn, Scotland, 2000.
12. Kelly, Douglas and Philip Rollinson, *The Westminster Shorter Catechism in Modern Wood*, Presbyterian and Reformed Publishing Co. Phillipsburg, NJ, 1966.
13. Kitov, A. E., *The Jew and His Home,* 5th ed., Shengold Publishers, New York, NY, 1963.
14. Lewis, C. S., *The Four Loves*, Harcourt Brace Jovanovich, New York, NY, 1960.
15. Luther, Martin, *The Small Catechism*, 1986 translation, Concordia Publishing House, St. Louis, MO, 1986.
16. Luther, Martin, *The Large Catechism of Martin Luther*, translated by Robert H. Fischer, Fortress Press, Philadelphia, PA, 1959.
17. *Luther's Small Catechism with Explanation*, Concordia Publishing House, St. Louis, MO, 1991
18. Meade, Starr, *Training Hearts, Teaching Minds, Family Devotions based on the Westminster Shorter Catechism*, Presbyterian and Reformed Publishing Co. Phillipsburg, NJ, 2000.
19. Munger, Robert Boyd, *My Heart, Christ's Home*, AMG Publishing, Chattanooga, TN, 1999.
20. Murray, John, *Divorce*, Baker Books, Grand Rapid, MI, 1972.
21. Nederhood, Joel, *The Splendid Journey,* C R C Publications, Grand Rapids, MI, 1998.
22. Schaeffer, Edith, *What is a Family*, Fleming H. Revell, Old Tappen, NJ, 1975.
23. Schoolland, Marian M., *Leading Little Ones to God, A Child's Book of Bible Readings*, Wm. B. Eerdmans, Grand Rapids, MI, 1962.

24. Williamson, G. I., *The Shorter Catechism for Study Classes*, 2 Volumes, Presbyterian and Reformed Publishing Co. Phillipsburg, NJ, 2000.
25. Wilson, Douglas J., *Reforming Marriage*, Cannon Press, Moscow, ID, 1995.
26. Wilson, Douglas J., *Standing on the Promises, A Handbook of Biblical Childrearing*, Cannon Press, Moscow, ID, 1997.

•••••

Scripture Index

18:19-20	84	4:16	201
18:20	80,112	8:14	160
18:35	218	8:15	210
19:17	193	10:2	111
21:5	186	11:2-4	215
22:37-40	194	11:4	218
25:23	193	11:13	215
25:31-46	167	12:15	86
25:41	208	15:24	63
25:41,46	184	18:1-8	55
26:26-28	212	18:22-27	160
26:38	186	22:44	188
26:39	217	23:43	192
26:41	218		
27:46	188		
28:19	180,212,213	John	
28:19-20	209	1:11-12	189
28:20	197	1:12	191,208
		1:14	162,185
		1:18	186
Mark		1:40-42	32
1:35	76	3:2	193
11:17	111,115	4:24	179
16:9	188	5:13	192
4:19	160	6:37,39	189
5:19	31	6:44-45	190
9:42	33	8:12	168
		8:39	57
		12:3-8	78
Luke		12:28	68
1:27,31,35,42	186	13:34-35	165
1:35	185	14:1-3	167
1:74-75	194	15:15	186
2:7	188	16:23	214
4:4	146	17:9,20	216

20:31	186	28:30-31	88

Acts		Romans	
1:8	30	1:16	210
1:11	188	1:21	195
2:7	194	1:25	195
2:24-27,31	188	2:14-15	193
2:37	190	3:9-21	207
2:37-38	206	3:20-22	185
2:38	213	3:24-25	191
2:38-39	213	4:6-8	191
2:42	197	5:1-2,5	192
2:42,46-47	209	5:8	52
3:21-22	186	5:10-20	184
5:42	88	5:12	27,183
8:36-37	213	5:17-19	191
10:24	31	5:20	19,23
11:18	209	6:4	212
12:5	215	6:4,6	191
12:12	88	6:17	109
15:14-16	187	6:23	184
16:15	32	7:7-8	206
16:28	204	8:1	191
16:31	31,140,141	8:15	215
17:31	188	8:17	191
18:8	31	8:18	104
19:19	54	8:30	190
20:7	200,201	9:5	185
20:7,9	201	9:22-23	180
20:20	55	10:1	216
20:21	208	10:5	193
20:32	210	10:13-17	210
20:35	70	11:36	178
26:18	199,210	12:9-13	166

1:22-25	108	1 John	
1:25	210	1:3-4	179
2:14-17	82	1:8,10	207
3:2-13	207	1:9	47
3:14,16	207	3:1	191,197
4:6	52,143	3:17	80
4:6-8	143	3:4	182
4:10	53	4	92
5:16	47	5:7	180
5:20	47	5:14	214,215
		5:16	207

1 Peter			
1:5	192	3 John	
1:10-12	186	12	206
1:15-19	194		
1:22	42		
2:1-2	210	Jude	
2:9	75,132	1:23	47
2:11	54		
2:17	202		
3:1	40	Revelation	
3:1-2	39,48	3:20	163
3:1-6	141	4:8	179
3:2	204	12:10-11	216
3:4	40	15:3-4	198
3:7	34,41,45,51	15:4	179
	112,140	21:8	43
3:21	211	22:20	216
4:9	80	22:20-21	219

2 Peter	
3:18	30